High-Interest/Low-Readability

Trendy Topics: Nonfiction

14 Reproducible Stories (12-Page Booklets, Each 5.5" x 8.5")
CD Includes: Word for Word Audio Tracks and PDFs of Storybooks and Activities
Featuring True Stories about Animals, People, Events, and Amazing Facts!

by
Jo Browning Wroe
and
Sherrill B. Flora

illustrated by
Julie Anderson

Publisher
Key Education Publishing Company, LLC
Minneapolis, Minnesota

CONGRATULATIONS ON YOUR PURCHASE OF A KEY EDUCATION PRODUCT!

Credits

Authors: Jo Browning Wroe & Sherrill B. Flora
Inside Illustrations: Julie Anderson
Editors: Claude Chalk & Karen Seberg
Page Design & Layout: Key Education Staff
Cover Design & Production: Annette Hollister-Papp
Voice Talent on CD: John Hoy, Cody Livingood & Sherrill B. Flora

About the Author of the Stories:

Jo Browning Wroe has taught both in the United Kingdom and in the United States. She earned her undergraduate degrees in English and Education from Cambridge University, Cambridge, England. She worked for 12 years in educational publishing before completing a Master's Degree in Creative Writing from the University of East Anglia, Norwich, England. Most of her time is now spent writing teacher resource materials and running workshops for others who love to write. Jo has been the recipient of the National Toy Libraries Award. She lives in Cambridge, England, with her two daughters, Alice and Ruby, and her husband, John.

About the Author of the Activities:

Sherrill B. Flora is the Publisher of Key Education. Sherrill earned her undergraduate degrees in Special Education and Child Psychology from Augustana College and a Master's Degree in Educational Administration from Nova University. Sherrill spent 10 years as a special education teacher in the inner city of Minneapolis before beginning her 20-year career in educational publishing. Sherrill has authored over 100 teacher resource books, as well as hundreds of other educational games and classroom teaching aids. She has been the recipient of three Directors' Choice Awards, six Parents' Choice Awards, seven Teachers' Choice Awards, and twenty-two Creative Child Magazine Awards. She lives in Minneapolis, Minnesota, with her two daughters, Katie and Kassie, and her very supportive husband, George.

Copyright Notice

Standard Book Number: 978-1-60268-103-3
Trendy Topics: NonFiction

Contents

How to Make the 14 Storybooks

Each of the fourteen, 12-page, 5.5" x 8.5" storybooks will be made from three 8.5" x 11" sheets of paper. Here is how you copy the reproducible pages and turn the story into a book:

STEP 1: 1st sheet of paper

Copy **cover/page 12** on the front and copy **page 2/page 11** on the back of an 8.5" x 11" sheet of paper. Fold it in half.

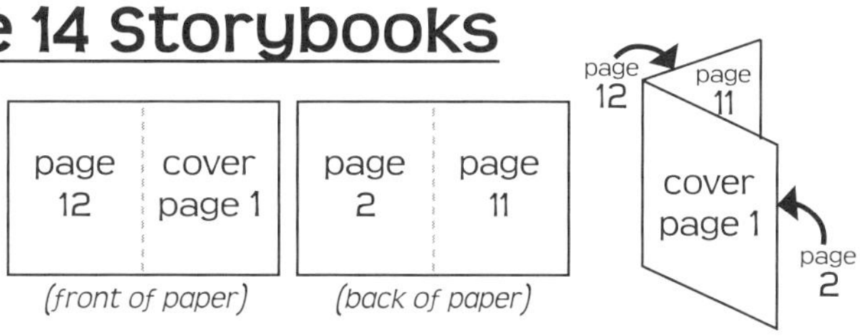

STEP 2: 2nd sheet of paper

Copy **page 10/page 3** on the front and copy **page 4/page 9** on the back of an 8.5" x 11" sheet of paper. Fold it in half.

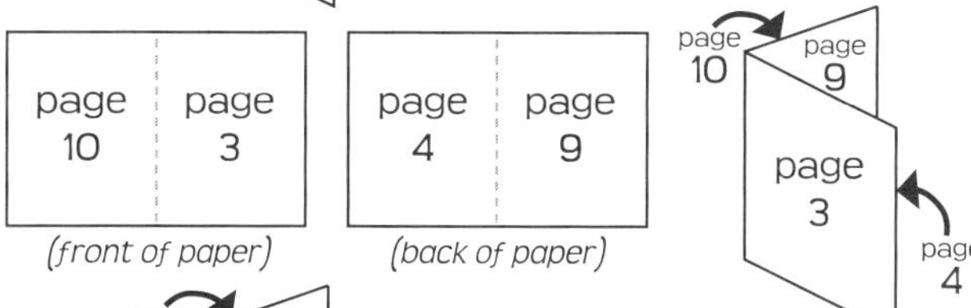

STEP 3: 3rd sheet of paper

Copy **page 8/page 5** on the front and copy **page 6/page 7** on the back of an 8.5" x 11" sheet of paper. Fold it in half.

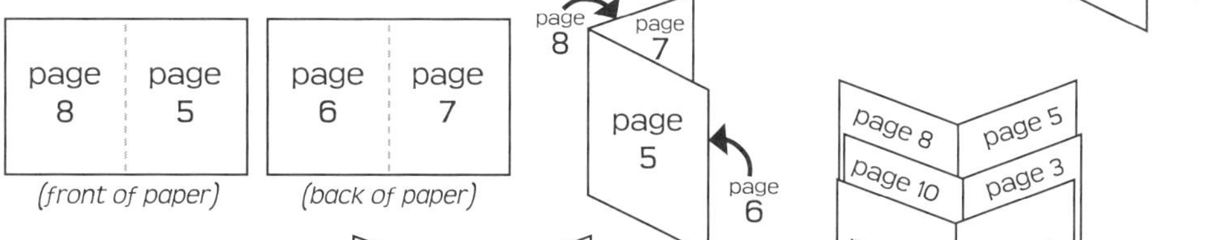

FINAL STEP:

After folding the three sheets of paper, put them together and staple on the fold.

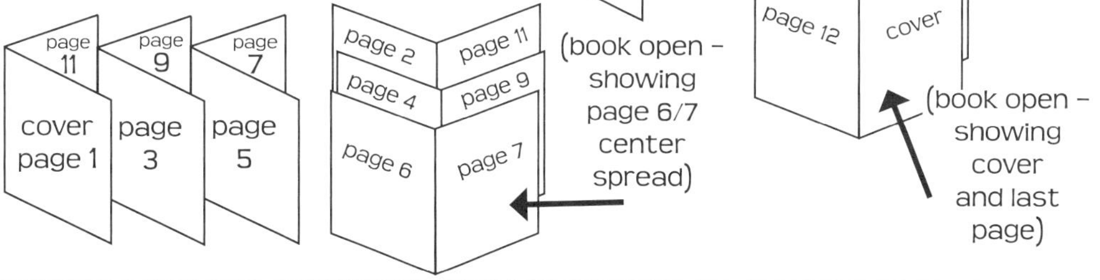

How to Use This Book

Who Is This Book Designed For?

Trendy Topics: Nonfiction has been written for students who are reading below grade level; for students who have reading disabilities, and for students who are reluctant or discouraged readers.

The Reproducible High-Interest/Low-Readability (and High-Quality) 12-Page Stories

Reading Levels: The engaging stories are written between early-second grade and early-third grade reading levels. Each story's specific reading level can be found below the story title on the **Table of Contents** (page 3). This information will help the teacher choose stories that are appropriate for the individual needs of the students. ***(Reading grade levels are not printed on any of the stories or on any of the reproducible activity pages.)***

Design of the Text: The style and size of font and the page layout have been designed to avoid impediments to fluency. Although the text may look the same as in any other book, the spacing between the lines has been increased, the font is larger and easier-to-read, and the ends of the sentences are found most often at the ends of lines in order to facilitate a return sweep. The larger font and simple sentence structure should help children feel more confident as they read.

Illustrations to Increase Text Comprehension: There is one illustration per two-page spread. The student will need to read the text in order to understand the story, yet the illustrations are there to provide picture clues that will help clarify the content.

Vocabulary Instruction

New and Difficult Story Vocabulary: There are new and sometimes difficult vocabulary words that are necessary for the content of each story. Prior to asking a student to read a story, review the story's word list on page 123 and then introduce and practice any unfamiliar words. Make flash cards of the new words and discuss what the words mean. Draw a picture of the word on each card to help students visualize the new vocabulary.

The Read-Along CD

Trendy Topics: Nonfiction comes with a CD featuring an audio track for each story. The students will hear some music and the title of the story. Then, the story is read on the CD exactly as it is printed on the student's copy of the story.

For many struggling readers, being able to listen to the story first can be extremely beneficial. Knowing the story's content ahead of time provides students with the opportunity to use context clues to help decode words and to interpret the meaning of the story. For other students, being able to track the text as they listen to the words allows for a valuable multisensory experience. Students can hear the words; they can see the words; and they can touch each word as they follow along while listening to the CD.

The Reproducible Activity Pages

Paper and pencil tasks are often "not fun" for struggling readers. There are three activities for each story. The first activity is a full page with many illustrations. The second page is divided into two activities. The teacher may choose to assign both halves of the page at once or cut the page in two and assign each half at different times. The diversity of the activities should encourage the students to finish and not become bored or frustrated.

Coloring, drawing, solving puzzles, and cutting and pasting activities have been included. These types of activities reinforce a wide range of reading skills and are often viewed as "more fun" by the students.

In short, *High-Interest/Low-Readability: Trendy Topics: Nonfiction* will provide your students with a complete reading experience.

Fill in the blanks. Use the Word Bank.

Word Bank: aye-ayes bugs cat cold hair long skin sleep stop tails warm

1. A Sphynx ________________ has no ________________.
2. All cats have oily ________________.
3. Sphynx cats get ________________ and can get sunburned.
4. Sphynx Cats like to ________________ with people to stay ________________.
5. Some people think that ________________ bring bad luck.
6. Aye-ayes have ________________, bushy ________________.
7. Aye-ayes teeth never ________________ growing.
8. Aye-ayes eat ________________ with their long fingers.

Let's draw a conclusion!

On another sheet of paper, answer this question. Do you think these two animals are "beauties" or are they "beasts"?

(Page 5)

Animals– Beauty or Beast?

(Page 6)

By day, aye-ayes sleep in trees in the rain forest. They curl up in nests of leaves. At night, they look for food. They tap on trees with their middle fingers. They can hear bugs move under the bark. Then, they scoop them out with those long fingers.

Why are they called aye-ayes? Maybe it's because that's the sound they make. Maybe it's what people say when they see one. With a mix of fear and shock, "aye-aye!"

What do you think? Beauties or beasts? Find some of your own and see what your friends think.

(Page 7)

Animals–Beauty or Beast?

When you see a spider, what do you think? "Let me get out of here!" Or, do you think, "Wow! How cool is that!"

Do you like Poodles or Great Danes? Do you like cats? Do you like cats with short hair? Do you like cats with long hair? Would you like a cat with no hair at all?

We all like different things. But, are there any really ugly animals? Are there animals that everyone would think are ugly? Well, what do you think of these animals?

(Page 8)

Another beauty or beast is the aye-aye. Aye-ayes come from an island called Madagascar. People on the island think they bring bad luck. Their eyes are dark brown or black. They have long, bushy tails and big ears. Their front teeth never stop growing.

Their fingers are long and thin with pointed claws. The middle finger is even longer than the rest.

People once believed that you might die if an aye-aye pointed a middle finger at you.

(Page 9)

First is the Sphynx cat. It has no hair. These cats look like they were made inside out! Their skin is the color their fur would have been.

Sphynx cats need to be washed — a lot. All cats have oily skin. Cats with fur use their fur to soak up the oil. So, if you don't wash a Sphynx cat, it will feel very greasy.

(Page 10)

With no fur, these cats get cold. They also get sunburned. They like to live indoors. People who love them say they make great pets. They love to cuddle.

They like to sleep under the covers next to a warm body. They have a loud purr. And, they are smart and "talk" a lot. But, I'm not sure I'd want to wake up next to one of them!

Name ____________________

Directions: Read the words in the boxes at the bottom of the page. Which words describe a Sphynx cat? Which words describe an aye-aye? Which words can be used to describe both of them? Cut out the word boxes along the dotted lines and glue them into the correct section of the Venn diagram.

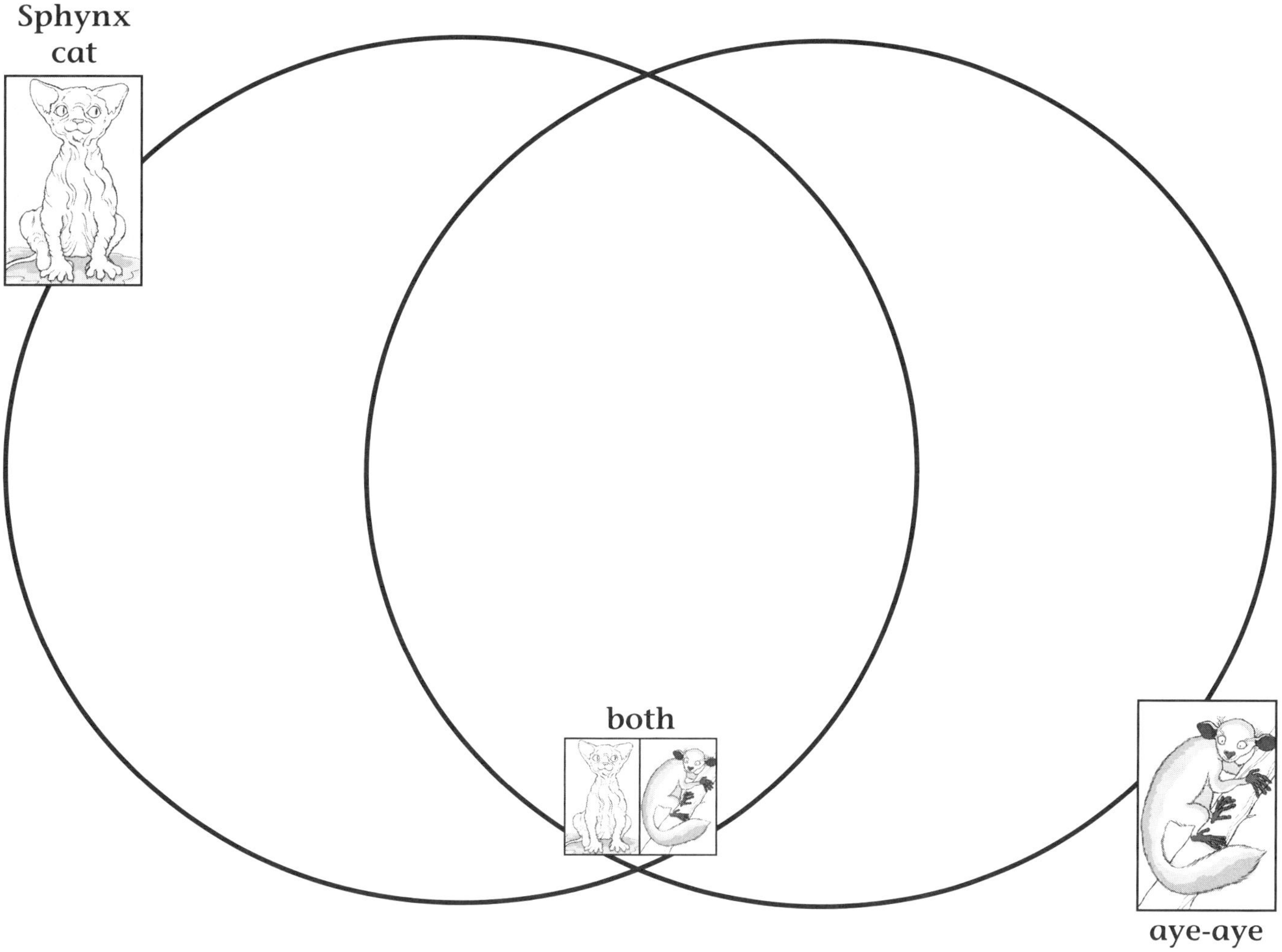

some people think it's ugly	has no fur	teeth never stop growing	some people think it brings bad luck
loves to cuddle	has two ears and claws	sleeps in trees	can get sunburned

Name ____

Directions: Circle the words from the Word Bank in the word search. The words may be horizontal or vertical.

Word Search

Word Bank
animals
aye-aye
beast
beauty
claws
pets
sleep
sphynx
tails
ugly

b	e	a	u	t	y	n	t	a
e	n	t	g	o	n	c	t	y
a	k	h	l	j	e	l	a	e
s	p	h	y	n	x	a	i	a
t	e	r	o	e	i	w	l	y
c	t	s	s	e	o	s	s	e
v	s	m	s	l	e	e	p	j
a	n	i	m	a	l	s	l	a

True or False

Directions: Read each sentence about the story. Write a "**T**" on the blank if the sentence is true. Write an "**F**" on the blank if the sentence is false.

1. All cats have oily skin. ________
2. Sphynx cats never need a bath. ________
3. Sphynx cats are smart and "talk" a lot. ________
4. Aye-ayes come from the Arctic. ________
5. Aye-ayes look for food at night. ________
6. Aye-ayes scoop up weeds with their tongues. ________

Fill in the blanks. Use the Word Bank.

Word Bank: animals brain dolphins fish flick hid human's play sharks trained trash

1. ________________ always seem to look happy.
2. Dolphins have saved people from ________________.
3. Dolphins love to ________________ with other ________________.
4. Humpback whales will ________________ dolphins off the end of their noses.
5. A dolphin's ________________ is the same size as a ________________.
6. Dolphins have been ________________ to pick up ________________.
7. A dolphin would get a ________________ when it brought the trainer some trash.
8. One dolphin ________________ trash so that it would get more fish.

Let's draw a conclusion!

On another sheet of paper, answer this question. What do you like most about dolphins?

(Page 13)

Nonfiction—Story 2

Dolphins

What's Not to Like?

(Page 14)

The dolphin had hidden a bag of trash! It was pushed in a corner by the pool filter. The dolphin saved the trash so that it could get fish from the trainer. But, that's not all.

The dolphin tore bits of trash off. It knew it would get a fish, even for a small bit. This way the dolphin could make its trash last longer! More fish for less work. That's what I call smart!

(Page 15)

Dolphins–
What's Not to Like?

Do you like spiders? Yes? Then, you're part of a small group. Most people say no. Most spiders can't hurt you. But, people are still scared of them.

On the other hand, if asked, "Do you like dolphins?" Most people would say a loud "yes!" Why is this?

(Page 16)

There are so many stories about how smart dolphins are. This is my favorite story. It's from a dolphin trainer at Marine World Africa USA. Trash in a dolphin pool is dangerous. So, dolphins were trained to pick it up. They'd do a tail stand and hand the trash to the trainer. The trainer would give them a fish.

One day the pool looked clean. But, the dolphin kept bringing trash for the trainer. So, another trainer got in the pool. He looked to see where the trash was coming from.

(Page 17)

For a start, dolphins look happy. Their wide, open mouths seem to smile at us. Also, they seem to like us. They like to swim alongside boats. It's as if they want to say hello. Dolphins have saved humans from sharks. They swim between the shark and the person. They don't leave until the people are safe.

We also like dolphins because they like to play. They surf waves in big groups. They even play with other animals. Humpback whales will flick them off the ends of their noses for fun.

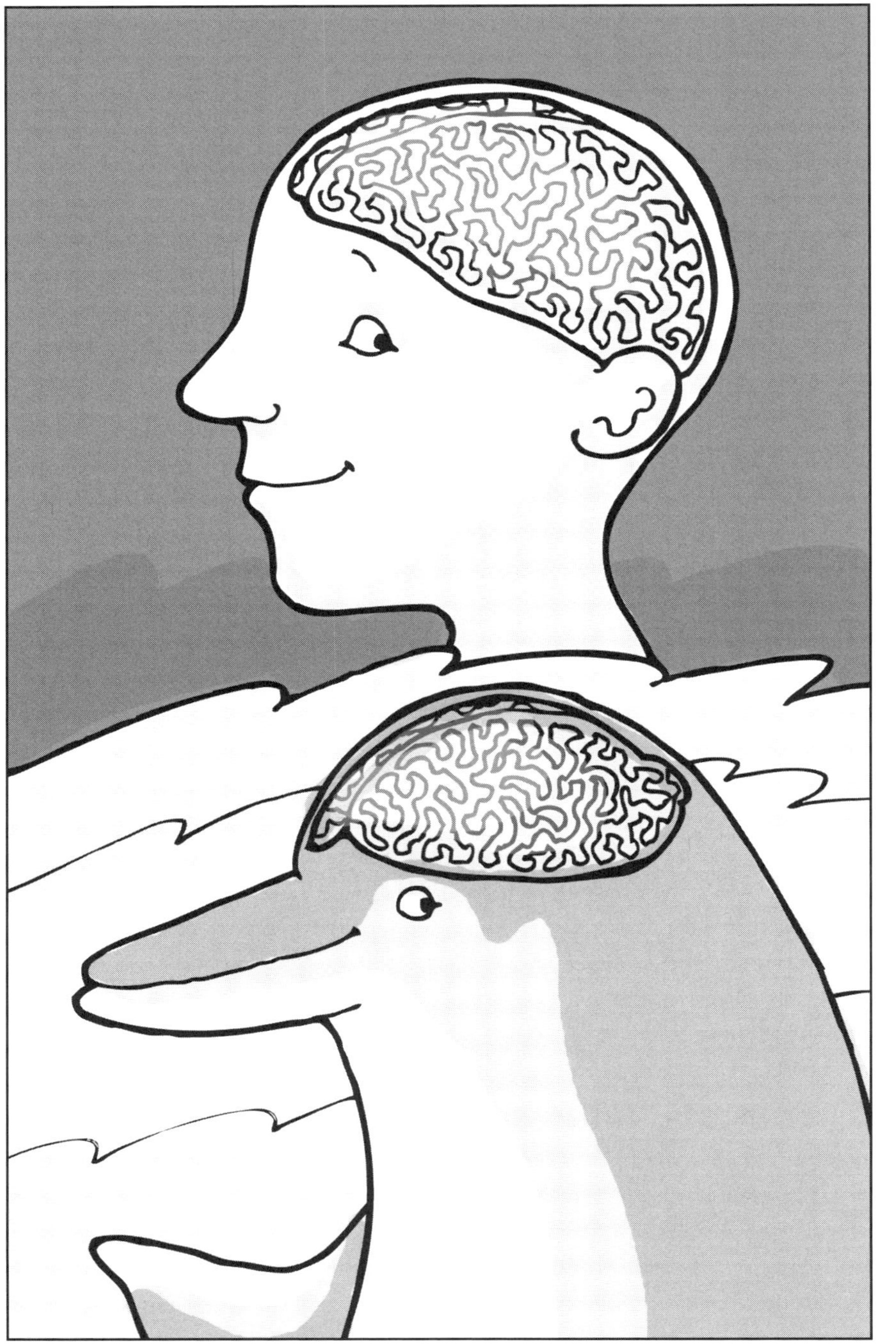

And, finally, maybe we like dolphins because they are so smart—just like us! Dolphins' brains are the same size as ours. Like us, their brains are split into two halves. They're called hemispheres.

Experts say that dolphins can use their two hemispheres better than we can. They can use each side one at a time. We can't. They can move each eye on its own. And, they can let one side of their brains sleep while the other side stays awake.

Name

Directions: This is a beach where people can see dolphins play. Follow the directions.

FOLLOW THE DIRECTIONS

1. Color one dolphin blue and the other dolphin gray.
2. Color the palm tree leaves green and the tree trunks brown.
3. Color the water blue.
4. Color the beach light brown or beige.
5. Color the sky light blue.
6. Draw stripes on the mom's swimsuit.
7. Color the girl's swimsuit pink.
8. Color the stripes on the dad's swimsuit green.
9. Draw pockets on the boy's swimsuit.
10. Draw some seashells on the beach.
11. Draw a bird in the sky.
12. Draw a lizard by the palm trees.

Name ______

Cause and Effect

Directions: A **cause** tells why something has happened, and an **effect** tells what happened. Draw a line from each cause in **Column A** to its matching effect in **Column B**.

Column A

1. Dolphins look happy,
2. A person can be saved from a shark attack,
3. The dolphin kept bringing the trainer trash,
4. A dolphin can use each side of its brain one at a time,

Column B

a. when a dolphin swims between the person and the shark.

b. and can move each eye on its own.

c. so most people like them.

d. so that it could keep getting fish.

Creative Writing

Directions: Make a list of the things that you would like to teach a dolphin.

Fill in the blanks. Use the Word Bank.

Word Bank:	clean	dead	eats	eel	no	one
	slime	teeth	ties	tongue	worm	

1. A hagfish looks like a ______________ or an ______________.
2. A hagfish has only ______________ nostril.
3. It has ______________ jaw.
4. Its ______________ has rows of ______________ on it.
5. A hagfish chews to get inside a ______________ fish and then ______________ its way out.
6. If a hagfish gets upset, it will ______________ you.
7. After a hagfish slimes something, it ______________ itself into a knot.
8. The job of a hagfish is to ______________ the ocean floor.

Let's draw a conclusion!

On another sheet of paper, answer these questions. Would you like a hagfish for a pet? Why or why not?

The World's Most Disgusting Animal

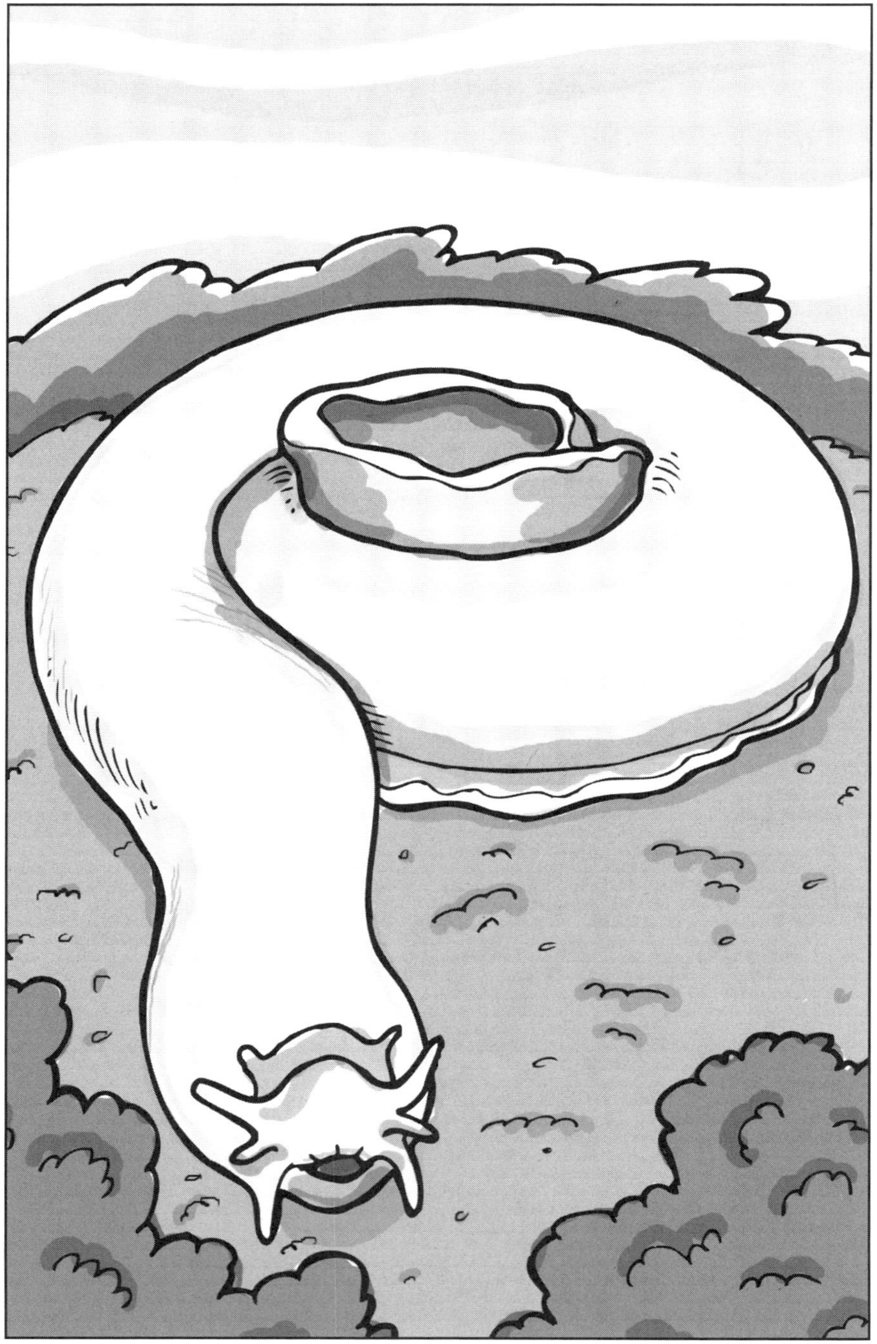

(Page 22)

What's more disgusting than a hagfish? Eating one! People in Asia think it is a treat. It costs a lot of money to eat them.

Why are there hagfish? Like most things, they have a job to do. Their job is to keep the ocean floor clean.

I'm glad hagfish do their job.

Still, I wouldn't want to touch one.

Or, eat one.

(Page 23)

The World's Most Disgusting Animal

Have you ever seen a hagfish? They are not pretty. They are not cute. Some say they are disgusting. What do you think?

The hagfish is not big or scary. It looks like a big worm or an eel. So, why is it so disgusting?

It's hard to know where to begin! The hagfish has only one nostril. It has no jaw. Its tongue has rows of teeth on it! That makes for a very strange face.

(Page 24)

Hagfish slime is not just any old slime. Hagfish slime smells bad. It's very sticky and very thick. But, that's not even the worst part. It's how much slime it makes. The slime oozes out of the pores on the hagfish.

One hagfish can turn five gallons (19 L) of seawater into gooey slime in seconds. The slime can kill other fish because they can't breathe. Sometimes, even the hagfish will die from its own slime. After a big slime, it ties itself in a knot. This squeezes the gooey slime off its body.

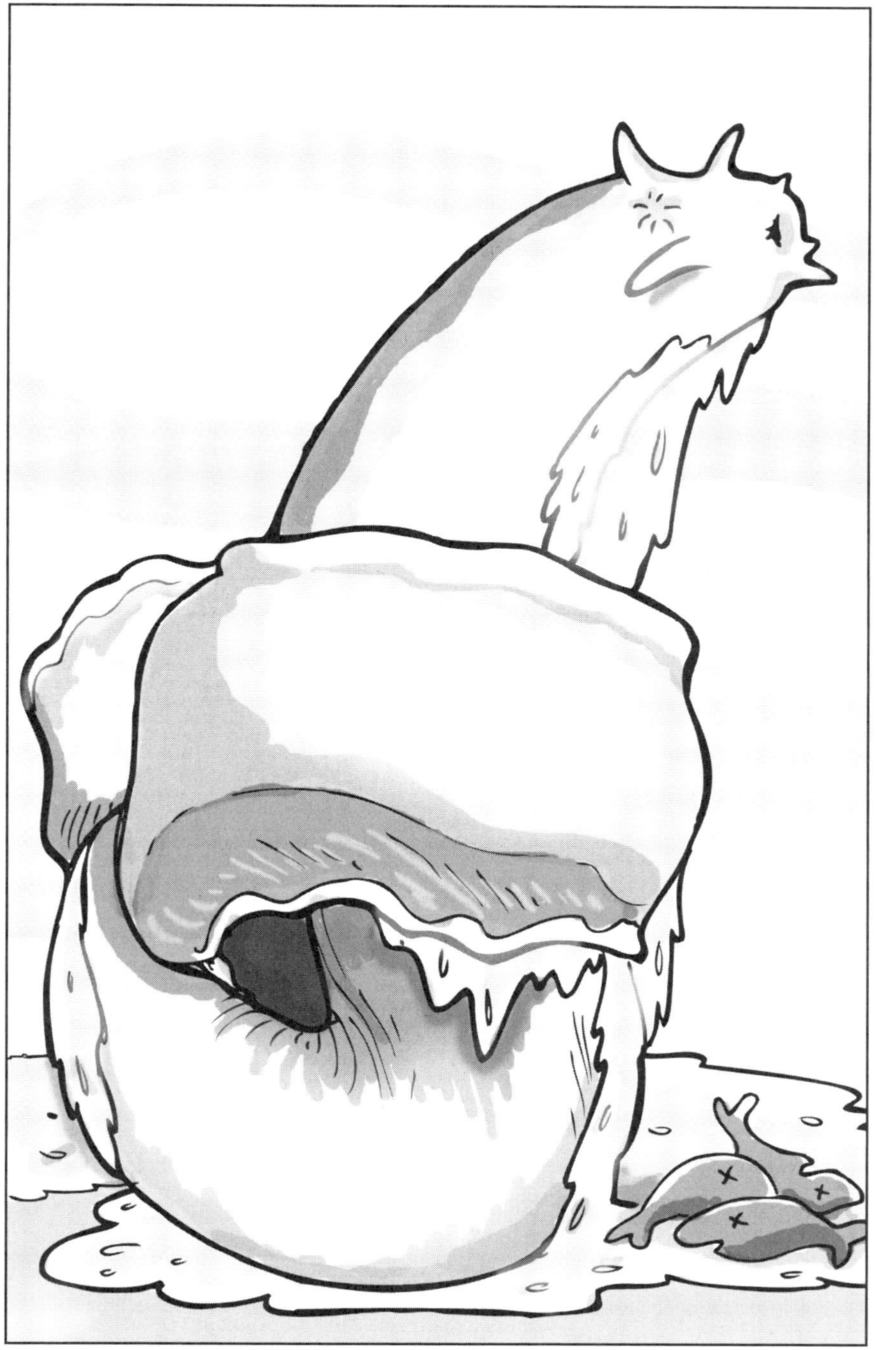

(Page 25)

Its eating habits are pretty gross too. Most fish eat other kinds of fish. That is no surprise. But, hagfish like to eat dead fish. Their dream menu is rotting fish! The hagfish slaps its toothy tongue on the dead fish. Then, it chews its way inside. When the hagfish is inside, it starts to eat.

Want one for a pet? I don't think so.

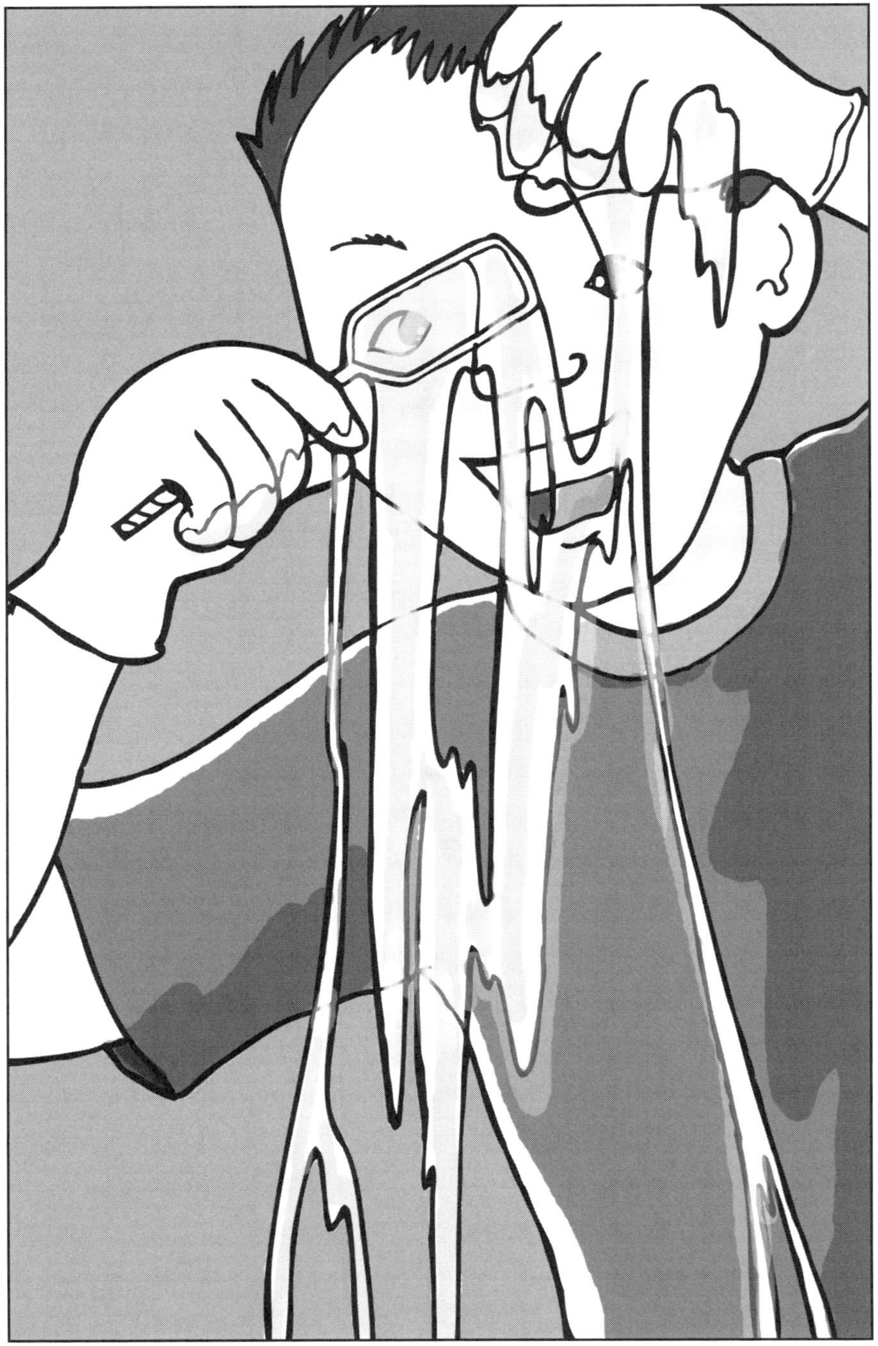

(Page 26)

Now you know a little about the hagfish. It has one nostril and teeth on its tongue. It eats dead fish from the inside out. Not very nice.
But, you know what? There's even more.

Here's a tip. If you ever meet a hagfish, stay calm. Make it think you are a friend. Play it nice music.
Tell it jokes. You must keep it happy.
If the hagfish gets upset, swim away!
You don't want to be near it.
It will slime you!

Name

Sequence

Directions: Read the sentences at the bottom of the page.
Cut them out along the dotted lines and glue them under the correct pictures.

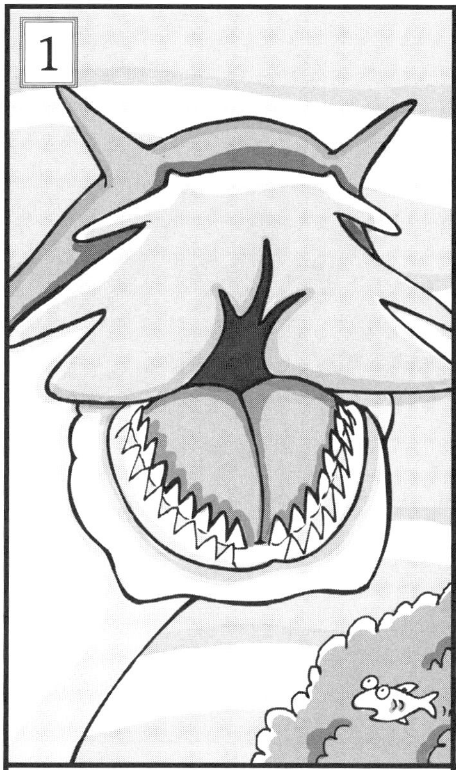

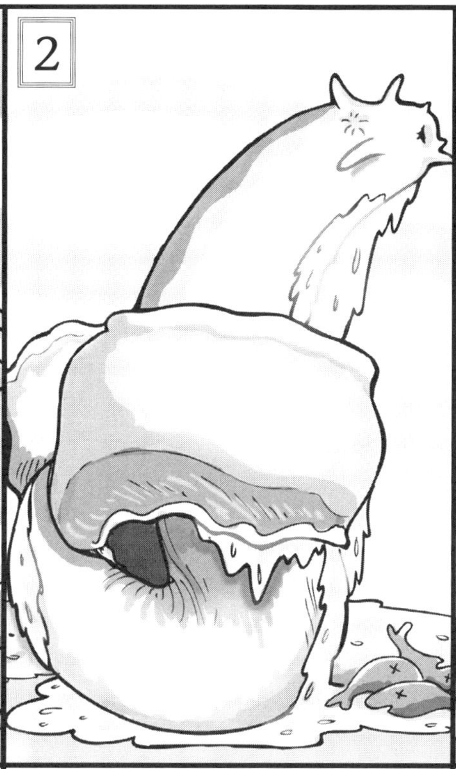

After a big slime, a hagfish ties itself in a knot. This squeezes the gooey slime off its body.

People in Asia think hagfish is a treat. It costs a lot of money to eat them.

A hagfish's tongue has rows of teeth on it! That makes for a very strange face.

Name

Creative Writing and Art

Draw a picture of a hagfish.	Write a sentence about it.

Directions: Circle **yes** or **no** for each sentence.

Drawing Conclusions

1. A hagfish looks like a big worm or an eel. **yes** **no**
2. The hagfish has three nostrils. **yes** **no**
3. Its tongue has rows of teeth on it. **yes** **no**
4. A hagfish's favorite food is rotting, dead fish. **yes** **no**
5. Other fish like to slime a hagfish. **yes** **no**
6. Slime oozes out of the pores on the hagfish. **yes** **no**
7. Hagfish do not cost very much money. **yes** **no**

Fill in the blanks. Use the Word Bank.

Word Bank: apple bed body bugs cold eat heat hide hurt itch red seed sting year

1. Sleep tight! Don't let the ________________ ________________ bite.
2. Bed bugs will ________________ your skin.
3. A bite from a bed bug does not ________________, but it might ________________.
4. Bed bugs only need to ________________ once a ________________.
5. After it eats, you can see a ________________ spot inside its ________________.
6. An adult bed bug is the size of an ________________ ________________.
7. Bed bugs like to ________________ in the springs of a bed.
8. Bed bugs don't like ________________ or the ________________.

Let's draw a conclusion!

On another sheet of paper, draw a picture of a bed bug and write a fictional story about one.

(Page 29)

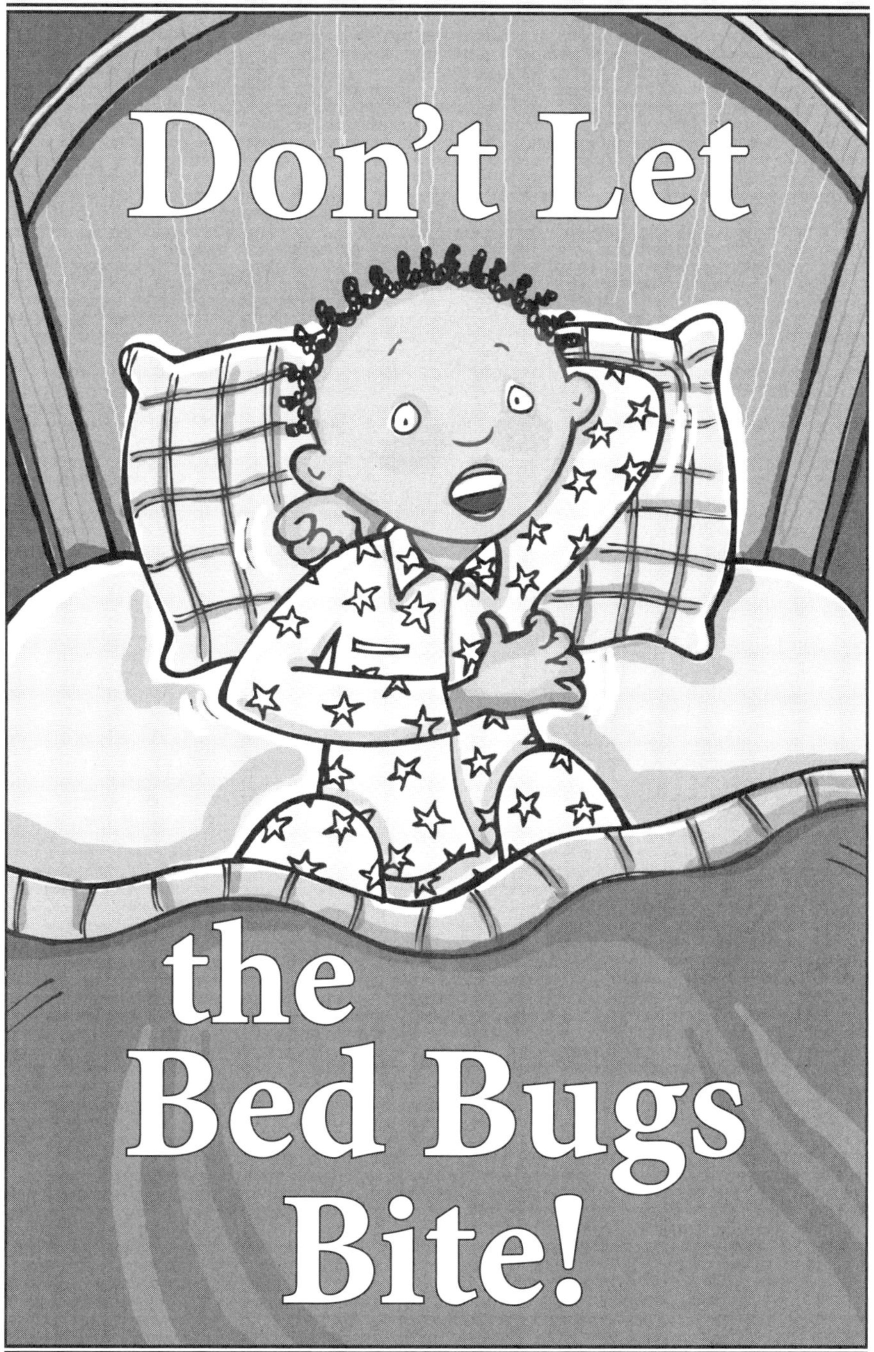

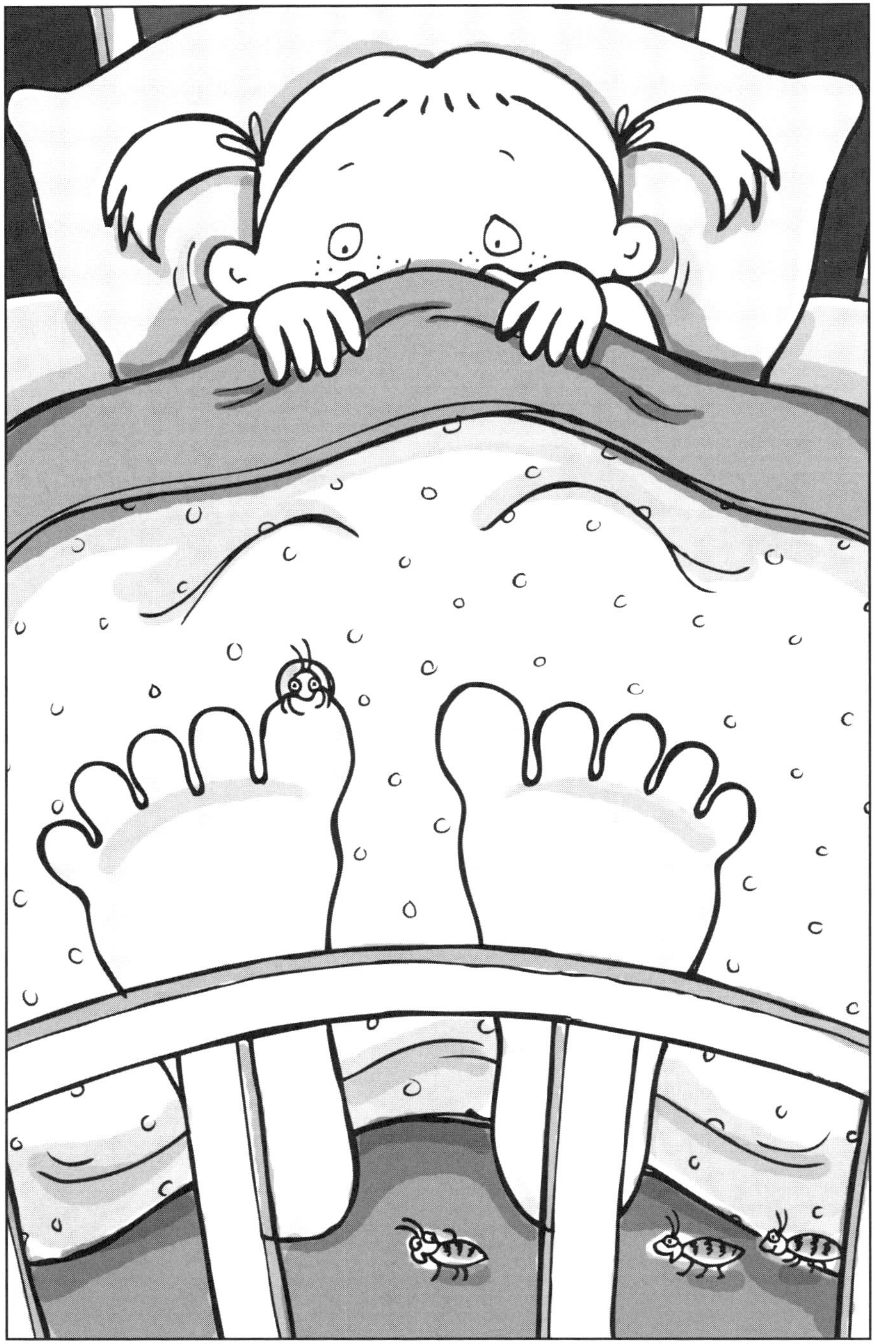

(Page 30)

Bed bugs are not dangerous.
But, would you like them in your bed?

If you have bed bugs, an expert can come and help. But, just in case, here are some things bed bugs don't like.

Heat - above 120 °F = 49 °C

Cold - below 32 °F = 0 °C

Vacuum cleaners

Washing machines

Mattresses wrapped in plastic (They can't breathe.)

"Sleep tight. I hope the bed bugs don't bite!"

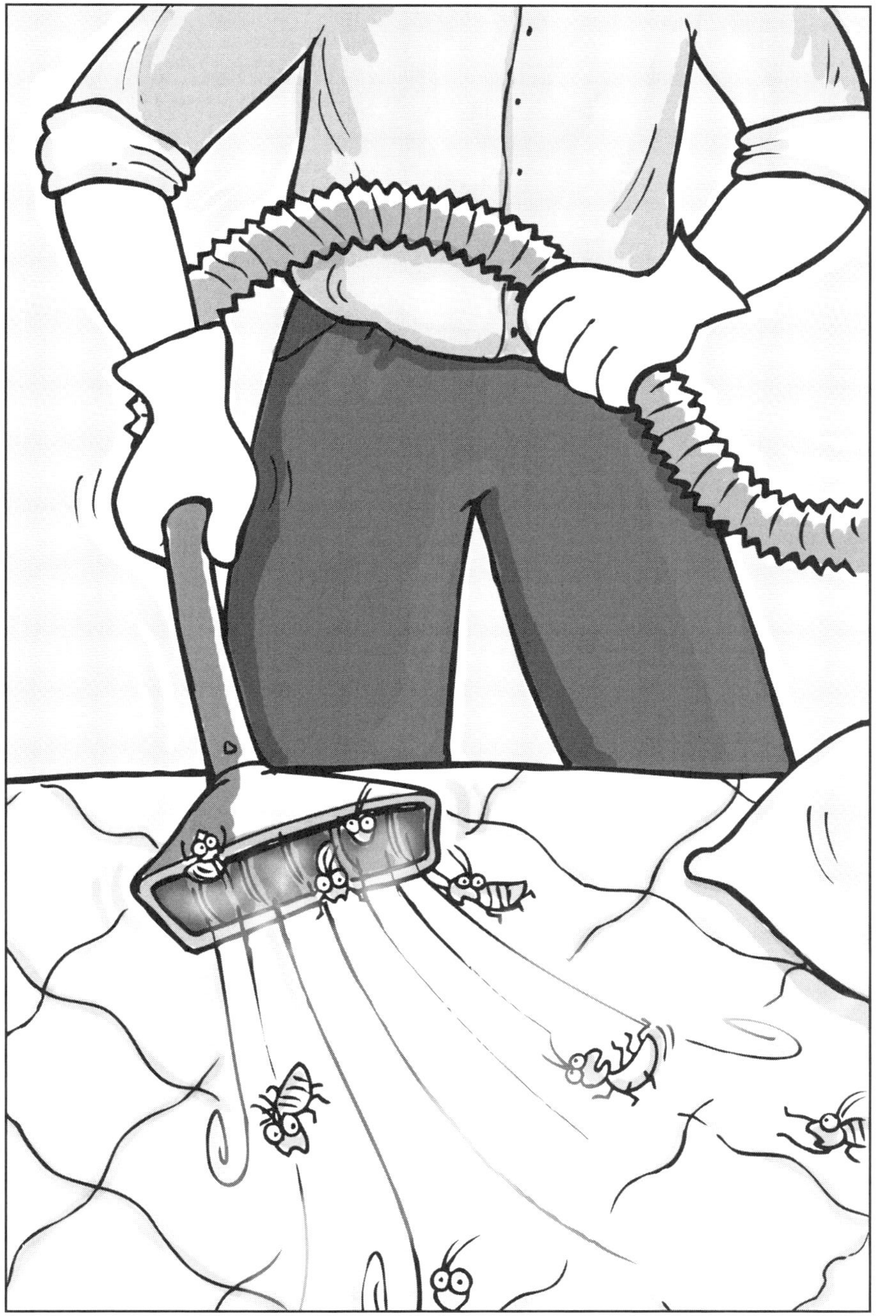

(Page 31)

Don't Let the Bed Bugs Bite!

Sleep tight. Don't let the bed bugs bite! Have you ever heard this? It's what people used to say to their children at bedtime. It's not a nice idea, is it?

Like mosquitoes, bed bugs sting your skin. Then, they suck your blood. But don't be too scared. Bed bugs don't pass on illness like mosquitoes. Their bites don't hurt. You won't even wake up. You might itch a little, but that's all.

(Page 32)

After World War II, we got rid of most bed bugs. We used an insecticide called DDT. DDT is not allowed any more. It hurts the environment.

This means that bed bugs are back! Bed bugs don't like dirt. They don't eat trash. They do like clutter though. The more clutter there is, the more places to hide. Bed bugs are good at hiding.

(Page 33)

Bed bugs can go for a year without eating! Even after all that time, it takes them only 10 minutes to fill up.
You can tell if a bed bug has eaten.
You can see a red spot inside its body.

So, what do bed bugs look like?
Well, a baby bed bug can hardly be seen. It's very tiny. An adult bed bug is the size of a small apple seed. They are red and brown and oval shaped. They have no wings. They are tiny and flat, and they are good at hiding.

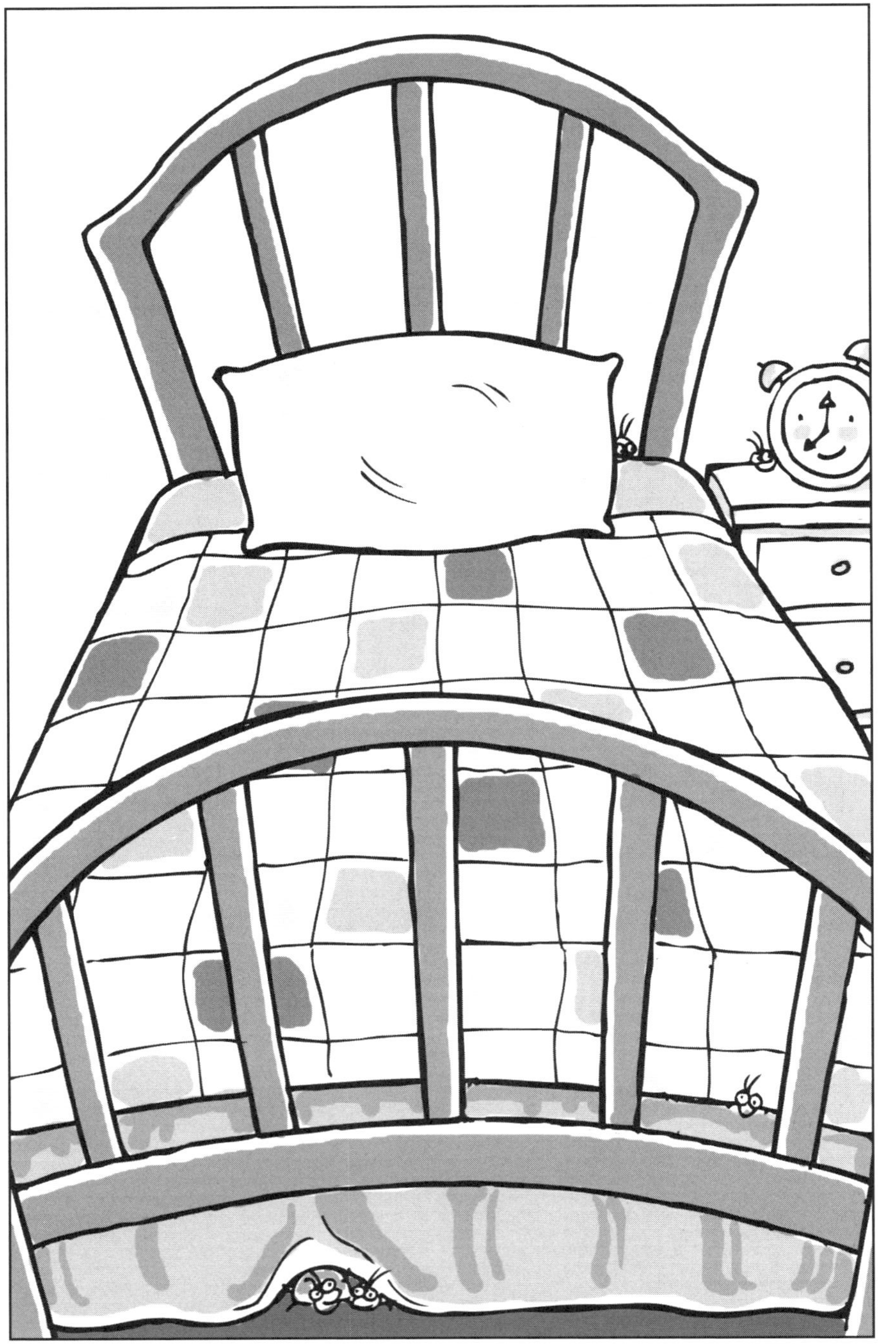

Why are they called bed bugs? Is it because they live in beds? Well, yes and no. During the day, they hide. They crawl into cracks or in the springs of a bed.

It's not beds that bed bugs like. It's the people in the beds. Bed bugs can't chase us! So, they like it when people are nice and still.

Name

Directions: Read the sentences at the bottom of the page.
Cut out each sentence and glue it under its matching picture.

1.

(glue here)

2.

(glue here)

3.

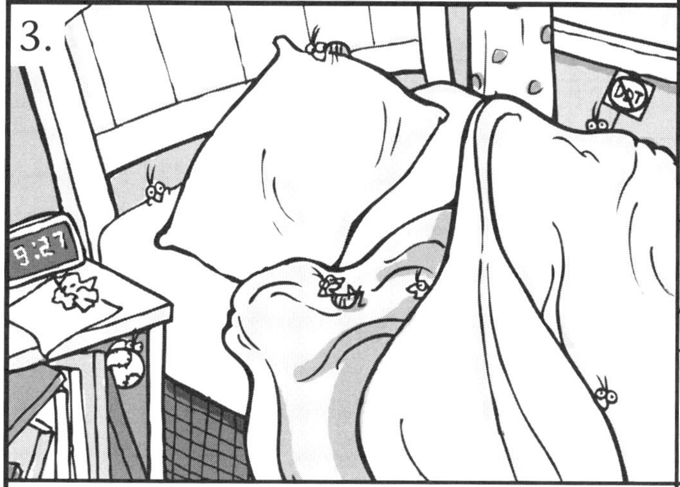

(glue here)

4.

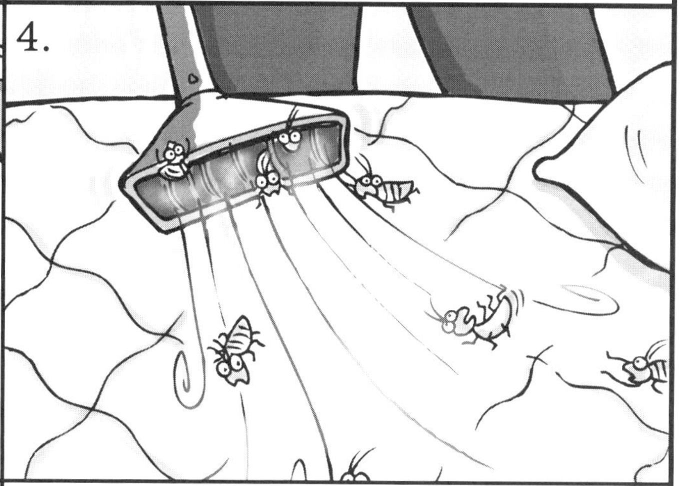

(glue here)

You can get rid of bed bugs with a good vacuum cleaner.	The bite from a bed bug will make a person itch.
If a bed bug has eaten, you can see a red spot in its body.	Bed bugs like to hide in cluttered places.

Name

Drawing Conclusions

Directions: Read the question in each box. Write your answer in each thought bubble.

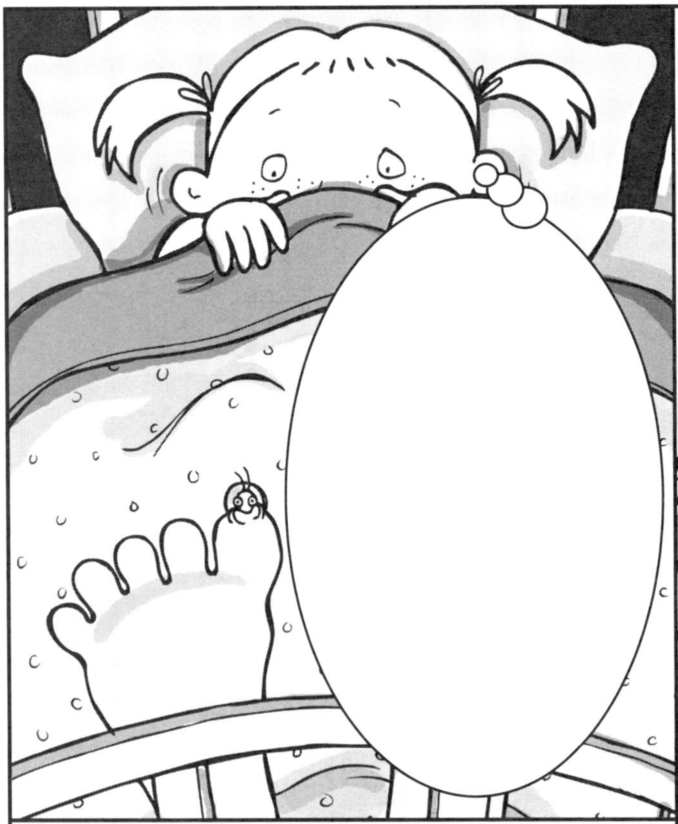

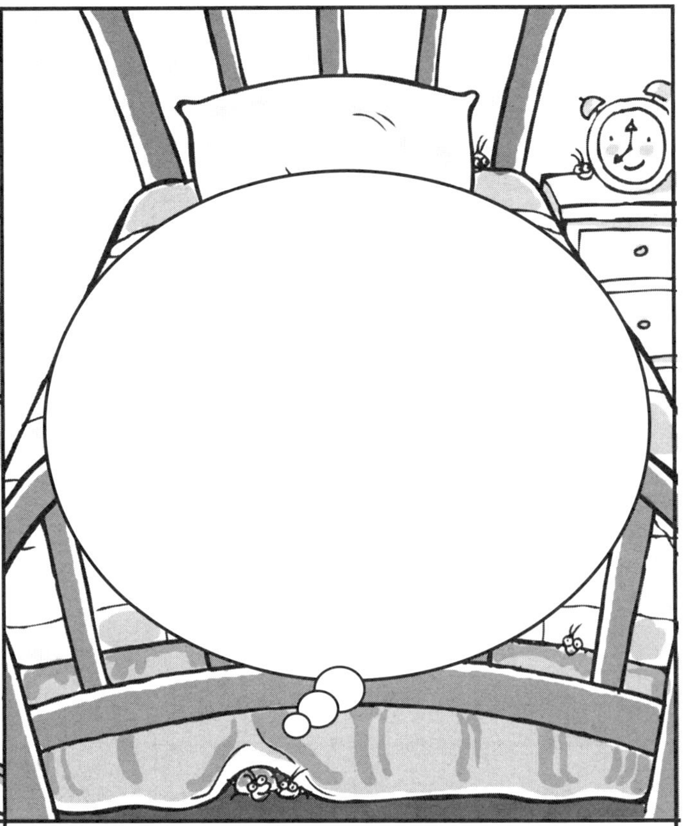

1. What do you think the girl is thinking?	2. What do you think the bed bug is thinking?

Main Idea

Directions: The **main idea** tells what the story is about. Read the following sentences and circle the sentence that you think best explains the main idea of the story.

1. Bed bugs became famous from the saying, "Don't let the bed bugs bite."

2. Bed bugs love to sleep in beds with people.

3. Learn all about bed bugs—where they live, what they eat, and how to get rid of them.

Fill in the blanks. Use the Word Bank.

Word Bank: Barry bristles caught coral England four giant reef worm jaws numb tank

1. A surprise happened at the Blue Reef Aquarium in ________________.
2. Something was attacking the ________________ reefs at the aquarium.
3. The staff took down the coral display and found a ________________ ________________ ________________.
4. The giant reef worm was ________________ feet long.
5. The giant reef worm has big ________________ and thousands of ________________.
6. A bristle sting can make you feel ________________.
7. The staff ________________ the giant reef worm, and it now has its own ______________.
8. The giant reef worm was named __________.

Let's draw a conclusion!

On another sheet of paper write a story about how the you think the Giant Reef Worm got into the aquarium in England.

(Page 37)

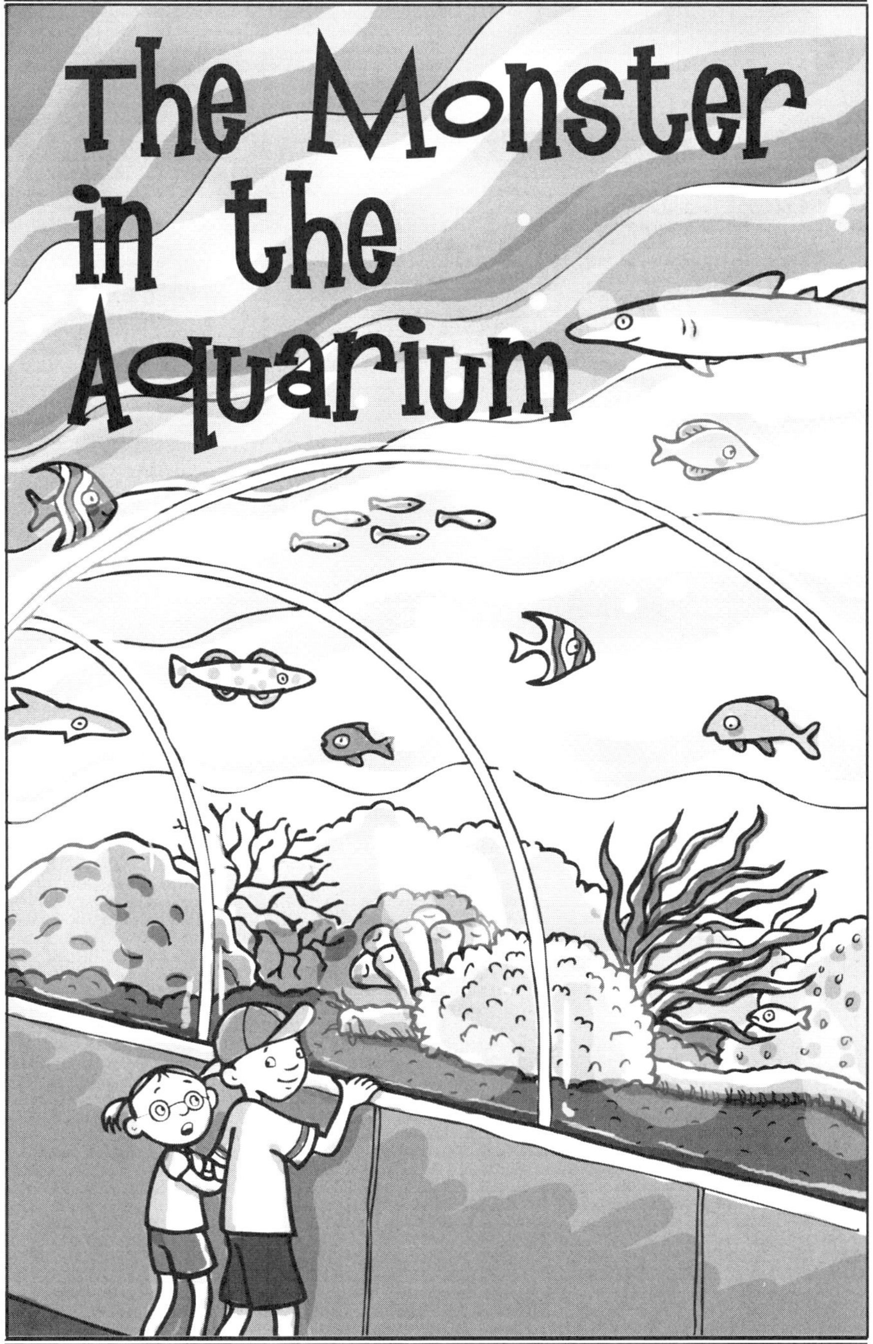

(Page 38)

The staff knew they could not pick the worm up. They got some scraps of fish. The giant reef worm didn't move for a long time. When it did, it bit right though a thick fishing line! The staff could not give up. At last, they caught it.

Now, the giant reef worm can be seen. It is safely in its own tank. Safe from the visitors — and the poor coral.

The staff had been upset about the coral. Yet, now they are fond of the giant reef worm. They have even given him a name—Barry.

(Page 39)

The Monster in the Aquarium

Kids love gross things. It's just the way it is. The staff at Blue Reef Aquarium in England knew this was true. They saw that kids liked the fish that did gross things. Starfish that throw up their own stomachs. Fish that eat their own poop.

"This is what kids like," they said. "Let's do a whole week just about them." The staff was having fun getting ready for this. But then, something else happened.

(Page 40)

How did a giant reef worm end up in England? The staff thought it must have come as a baby. It must have come with coral from the ocean. It looked like it was from a horror movie.

The giant reef worm had big jaws. It was covered in bristles — thousands of bristles. If they stung you, you'd really know it! The bristles would make your body numb. You might never get the feeling back.

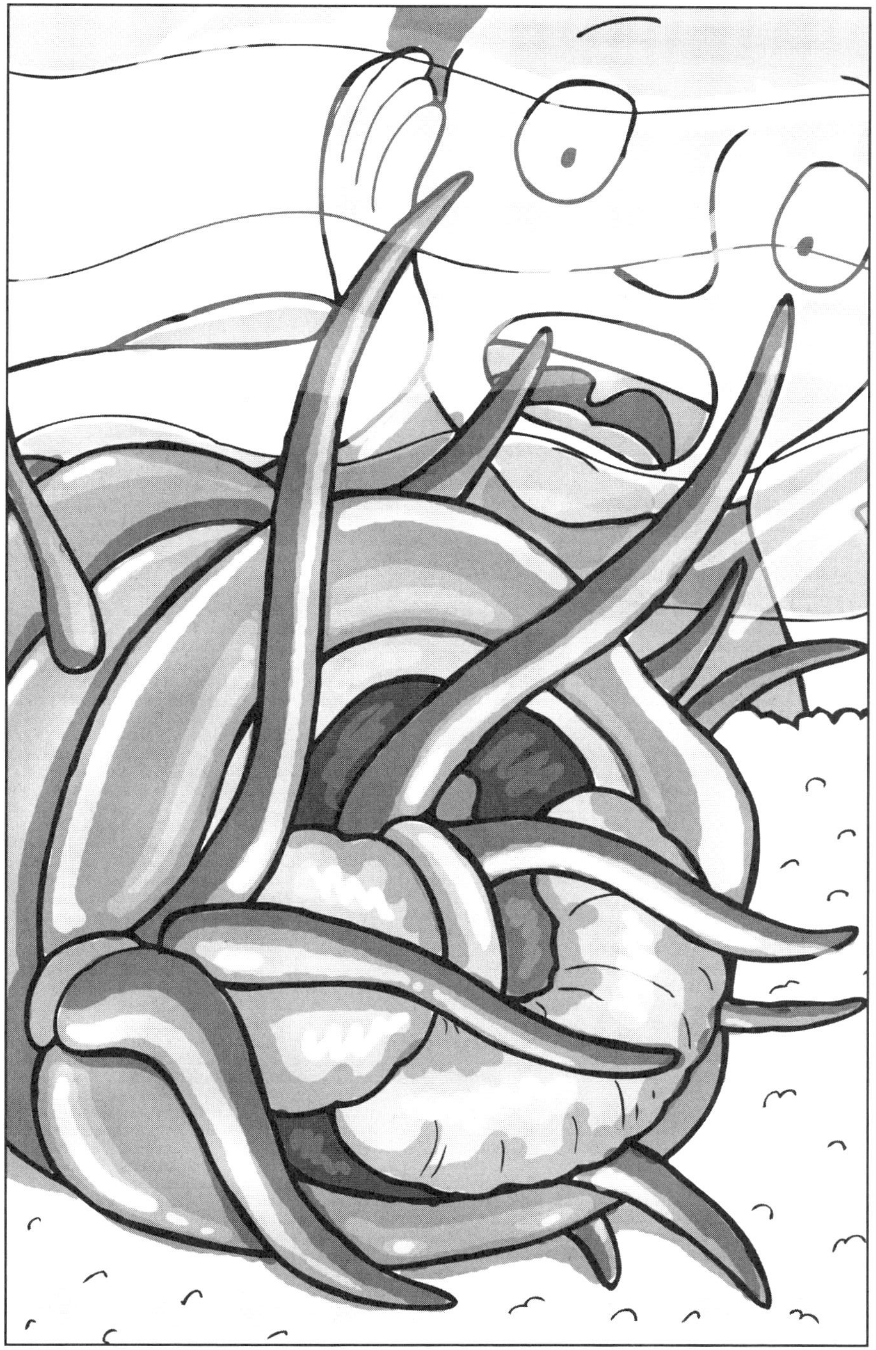

(Page 41)

At the aquarium, they grow coral reefs. The reefs grow very slowly. It's worth the wait. They are very beautiful. The staff was proud of their coral.

Then, disaster struck. The corals were attacked! Some were even cut in half. Who or what was doing this? The staff took turns keeping watch. No one saw anything. But, the coral kept being hurt.

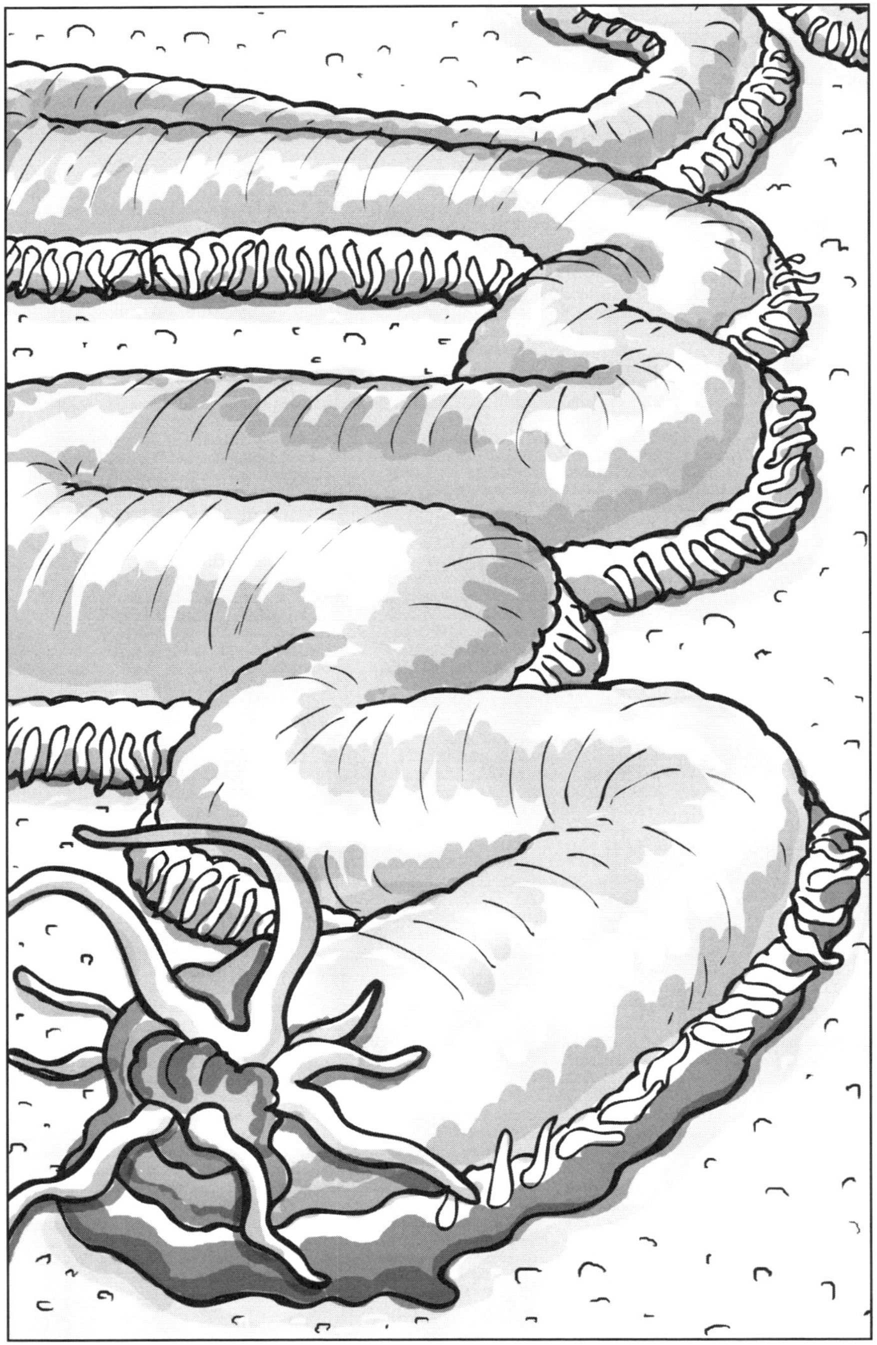

There was only one thing to do. The display had to be taken down—rock by rock. This was a hard thing to do. But, they soon found out that it was the right thing to do!

When half the rocks had been taken down, they found it. They found what had been eating their coral! It was a four-foot-long, giant reef worm!

Name

Directions: Read the question in each box. Write your answer in each speech bubble.

1. What do you think the kids are thinking?

2. What do you think the girl is saying?

3. What do you think the Giant Reef Worm is thinking?

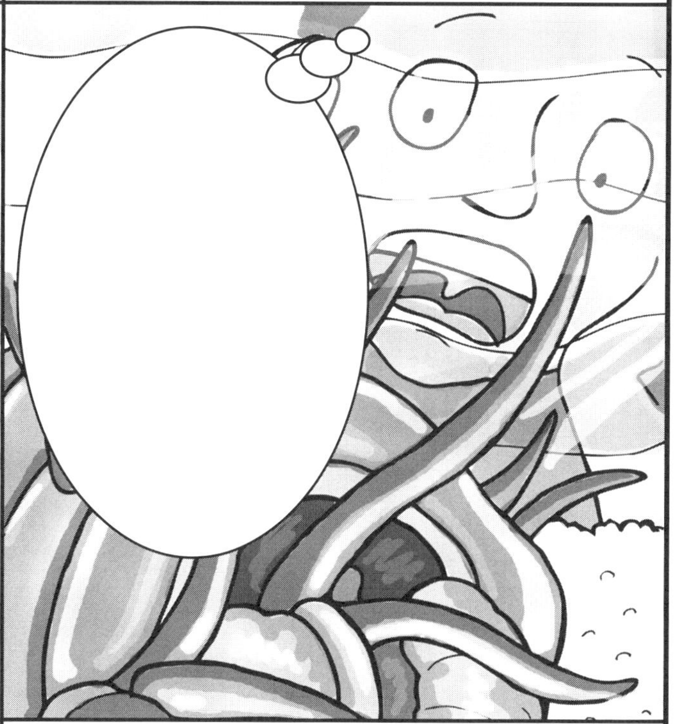

4. What do you think the boy is thinking?

Name

Creative Writing

Directions: Pretend you are a reporter for the newspaper. What two questions would you ask about the giant reef worm?

1.

2.

Cause and Effect

Directions: A **cause** tells why something has happened, and an **effect** tells what happened. Draw a line from each cause in **Column A** to its matching effect in **Column B**.

Column A

1. Because the staff at the aquarium in England knew kids liked fish that did gross things,
2. The coral was being attacked,
3. They took down half the rocks and
4. If a giant reef worm stings you

Column B

a. so the staff took turns keeping watch.

b. found the four foot giant reef worm.

c. your body will become numb.

d. they planned to do a whole week about them.

Fill in the blanks. Use the Word Bank.

Word Bank: beds bladder Bruiser buy dogs five less necklaces purse sleeves small washed

1. ________________ was one of the first famous purse ________________.
2. People like to ________________ things for the purse dogs.
3. You can buy ________________ and travel ________________ for these dogs.
4. Most purse dogs weigh ________________ than ________________ pounds.
5. The dogs have to be ________________ to fit in a ________________.
6. A purse dog also has tiny insides and a tiny ________________.
7. Be sure to buy a purse that can be ________________.
8. In Roman times, ladies used their ________________ to carry their small dogs.

Let's draw a conclusion!

On another sheet of paper, answer this question. What breed of small dog would you like? Research and make a list of the dog's personality traits.

Bruiser may have made purse dogs big in the United States. But they are not really such a new thing. Rich women have always made a fuss over their dogs. In Roman times, they carried them in their large sleeves. Do you think they were called "sleeve dogs" back then?

Some people don't like the idea of purse dogs. They say these dogs are animals, not fashion items. They think the dogs look unhappy. What do you think?

(Page 47)

Purse Dogs

Have you seen the movie *Legally Blonde?* If you have, you'll know Bruiser. Bruiser is a Chihuahua. He goes to Harvard Law School with his owner, Elle Woods. She takes him everywhere in her purse. This is a first at Harvard!

The film was made in 2001. A few years later, purse dogs became all the rage. Britney Spears, Jessica Simpson, and Paris Hilton all have one. You even see the tiny dogs on the red carpet with their famous owners. People with purse dogs like to buy things for them. You can get necklaces, charms, collars, and hair barrettes.

Would you like to have one in your purse? If so, there's something you need to know. This is very important. It's not just the outside of the dog that's super small. It's their insides too. Their hearts are tiny. Their stomachs are tiny. Their lungs are tiny.

And, so are their bladders! A purse dog can't hold on for very long. When it needs to go, it needs to go! And, that might be in your purse! Make sure to get a purse that's easy to wash.

(Page 49)

They all come in super tiny sizes. You can also buy travel beds, car seats, and travel bowls. These dogs need a lot of stuff!

Paris Hilton's dog is called Tinkerbell. She may be the world's best dressed purse dog. Paris now has her own line of dog clothes.

(Page 50)

Purse dogs have to be small (to fit in your purse). They have to be light (so you can carry them all day long). Most of them weigh less than five pounds (2.27 kg). So, what breeds of dogs can fit in your purse?

Teacup poodles

Pomeranians

Yorkshire Terriers

Maltese

Bichon Frise

Chihuahuas

Name

Visual Discrimination

Directions: Read the names of the dogs at the bottom of the page.
Cut them out along the dotted lines and glue them under the correct pictures.
Use an encyclopedia if you need additional help.

(glue here)

(glue here)

(glue here)

(glue here)

(glue here)

(glue here)

Teacup Poodle	Chihuahua	Maltese
Pomeranian	Yorkshire Terrier	Bichon Frise

Name

Directions: Read each question.
Circle the correct answers.

Comprehension

1. What was the name of the dog in *Legally Blonde?*

   a. **Bruiser**

   b. **Tinkerbell**

   c. **Johnson**

2. What is the name of Paris Hilton's dog?

   a. **Bruiser**

   b. **Tinkerbell**

   c. **Johnson**

3. Most purse dogs weigh less than how many pounds?

   a. **3 pounds**

   b. **4 pounds**

   c. **5 pounds**

4. Where did some women carry their dogs in Roman times?

   a. **tote bags**

   b. **sleeves**

   c. **carts**

Directions: Make a list of all the things you would buy if you had a dog that fit in a purse.

Creative Writing

Fill in the blanks. Use the Word Bank.

Word Bank: Antarctica chicken claws crest feet fishing food not ten three

1. The *Cryolophosaurus* was about 20 ________ (6m) long.
2. Experts think *Cryolophosaurus* was from ________.
3. The *Cryolophosaurus* had a ________ just like a ________.
4. *Tanystropheus* was small but had a neck that was ________feet (3m) long.
5. Experts think *Tanystropheus* used its neck as a ________ pole.
6. *Therizinosaurus's* ________ were ________feet (91 cm) long.
7. *Therizinosaurus's* claws were ________ good for fighting.
8. Its claws were probably used for getting ________.

Let's draw a conclusion!

On another sheet of paper, answer this question. What is your favorite animal? Draw a picture of it and make a list of facts about it.

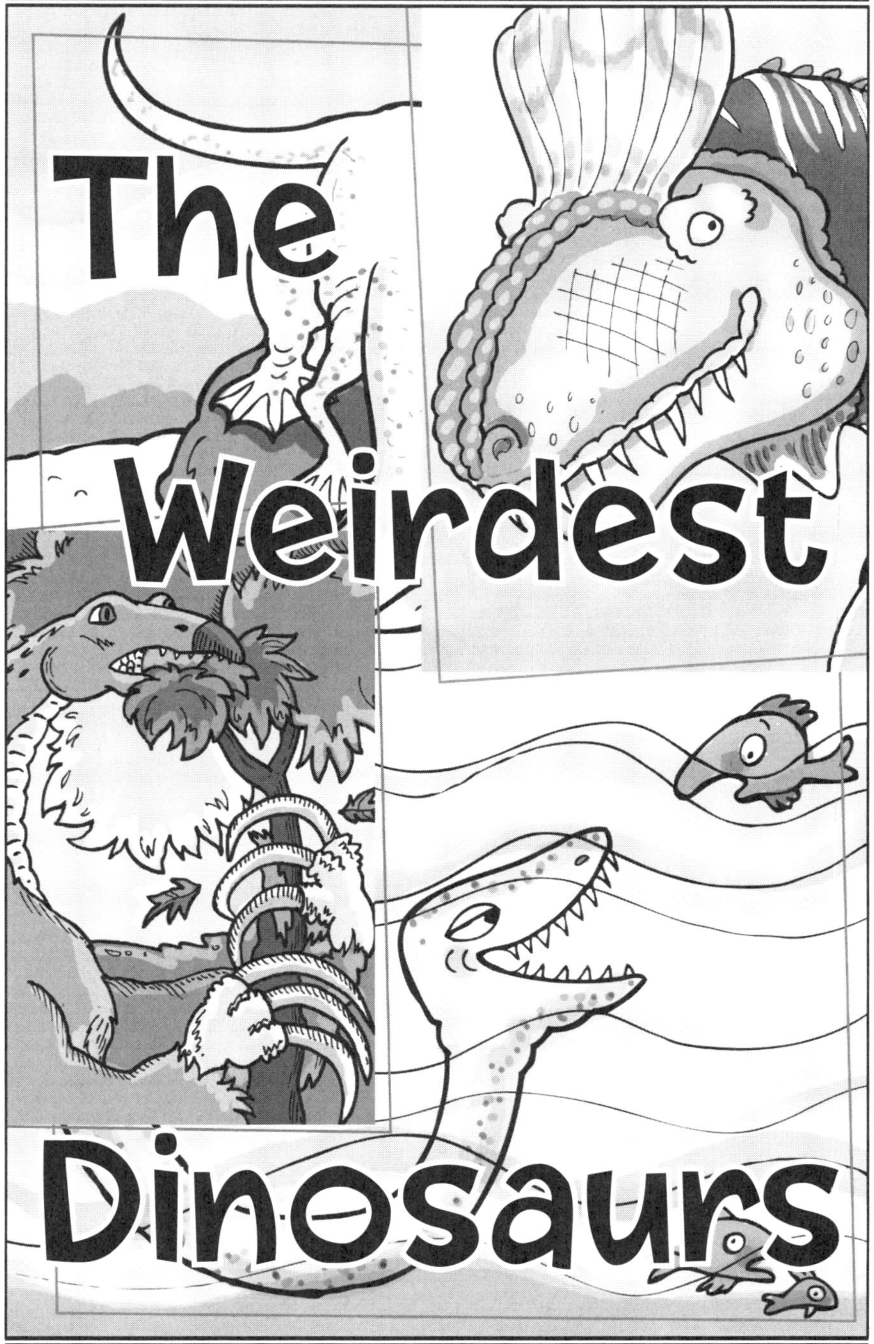

(Page 54)

Last but not least is the *Therizinosaurus.* Cross Big Bird with Count Dracula. That's the *Therizinosaurus.* You've got to admit, that's a bit weird. This dinosaur was 30 feet (9m) long and weighed 3 tons (2.722 kg). It had a squat body, long neck, and a tiny head — normal dinosaur stuff.

What makes it stand out are its claws. It had three on each arm. And they were huge — three feet (91 cm) long. The claws look fierce, but they weren't any good for fighting. They were too big. More likely they were used to reach up into trees to get food. They might also have been used to attract a mate.

What's your weirdest dinosaur?

The Weirdest Dinosaurs

All dinosaurs look weird.
That's one of the reasons we like them.
But, some of them stand out as
even weirder than the others.
Read about three pretty strange ones.
You might even have your own favorite.

(Page 56)

Number two on the list is actually a reptile. *Tanystropheus* looks like it came out of a cartoon. This creature was 20 feet (6 m) long and weighed about 30 pounds (14 kg). Some experts think it only ate fish. Its body was like a living fishing pole! It's body was 5 feet (1.5 m) long. That's like a small human body. But, wait for this. Its neck was over 10 feet (3 m) long. It also had webbed feet.

Experts think the reptile spent its days doing one thing —sitting on a rock near a river. When it saw a fish, it put its head in the water and grabbed it.

(Page 57)

Cryolophosaurus was 20 feet (6 m) long. It ate meat. We are not sure how heavy it was. Some experts think it might have weighed 1,025 pounds (465 kg).

This fella makes the top three on two counts. First, it's one of the few dinosaurs from Antarctica. You would think it needed fur to keep warm. But, this was a long, long time ago. We think that back then, Antarctica was not below freezing like it is today.

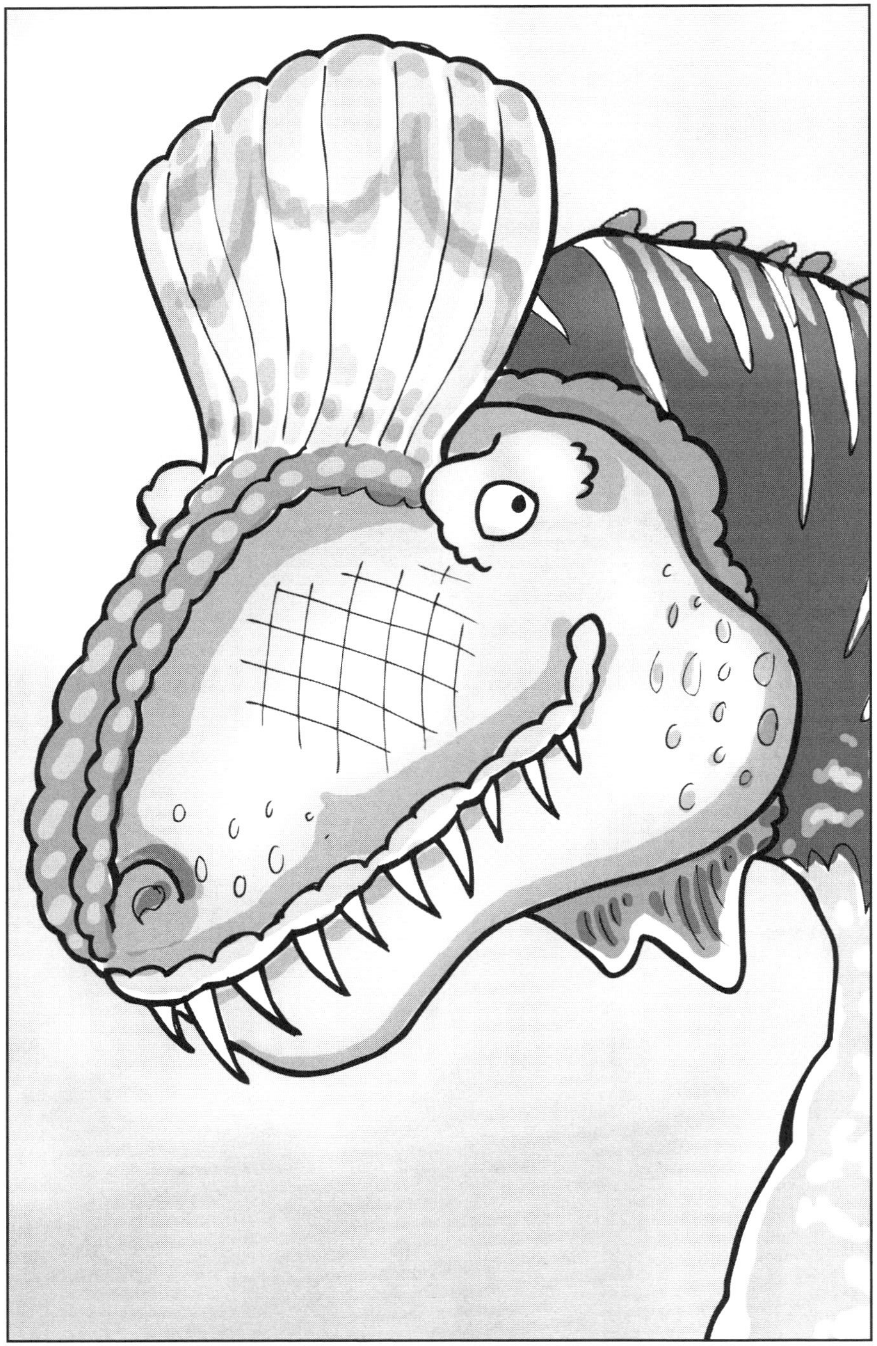

Second, it had a crest like a chicken. But, it was an odd crest. Most crests run from the front to the back. This one ran from ear to ear, across the head.

Cryolophosaurus was found in the 1990's. Because of its crest, they gave it a funny name. It was called Elvisaurus! Maybe this makes it the coolest dinosaur.

Name

Directions: Choose a word from the Word Bank to answer each crossword question. Write the answer in the correct word boxes.

1. 2. 3.
4. 5.
6.

Word Bank

chicken claws cool
dinosaur neck read

ACROSS

4. *Cryolophosaurus* was a _______.
6. One reptile had a very long _______.

DOWN

1. One dinosaur had a head that looked like a __________.
2. Elvisaurus was one ________ dinosaur.
3. Another dinosaur had huge ________.
5. You can ________ all about dinosaurs.

Name

Creative Art

Directions: Draw a picture of your favorite dinosaur.

True or False

Directions: Read each sentence about the story. Write a "**T**" on the blank if the sentence is true. Write an "**F**" on the blank if the sentence is false.

1. *Cryolophosaurus* was one of the few dinosaurs from Antarctica. ________
2. *Cryolophosaurus* had a crest that ran from ear to ear. ________
3. *Tanystropheus* looked like a duck. ________
4. *Tanystropheus* had a neck that was 10 feet (3 m) long. ________
5. *Therizinosaurus* had three arms. ________
6. *Therizinosaurus* was huge—30 feet (9 m) long and it weighed 3 tons. ________

Fill in the blanks. Use the Word Bank.

Word Bank: color eight energy fangs feet fight rattle snakes spit venom

1. Some snakes ________________ by biting.
2. 450 types of ________________ have poisonous ________________.
3. It takes ________________ to make venom.
4. To get out of trouble some snakes make a ________________ sound.
5. Other snakes can change their ______________.
6. A spitting cobra can ________________ its venom up to ________________ feet (2 m).
7. Some snakes can fold their ________________ in their mouths.
8. A cobra can grow 18 ________________ (5.5 m) long.

Let's draw a conclusion!

On another sheet of paper, answer this question. The booklet ends with the sentence, "To a snake, you're a waste of venom." What do you think this sentence means?

(Page 61)

Nonfiction—Story 8

It Slithers—Snakes

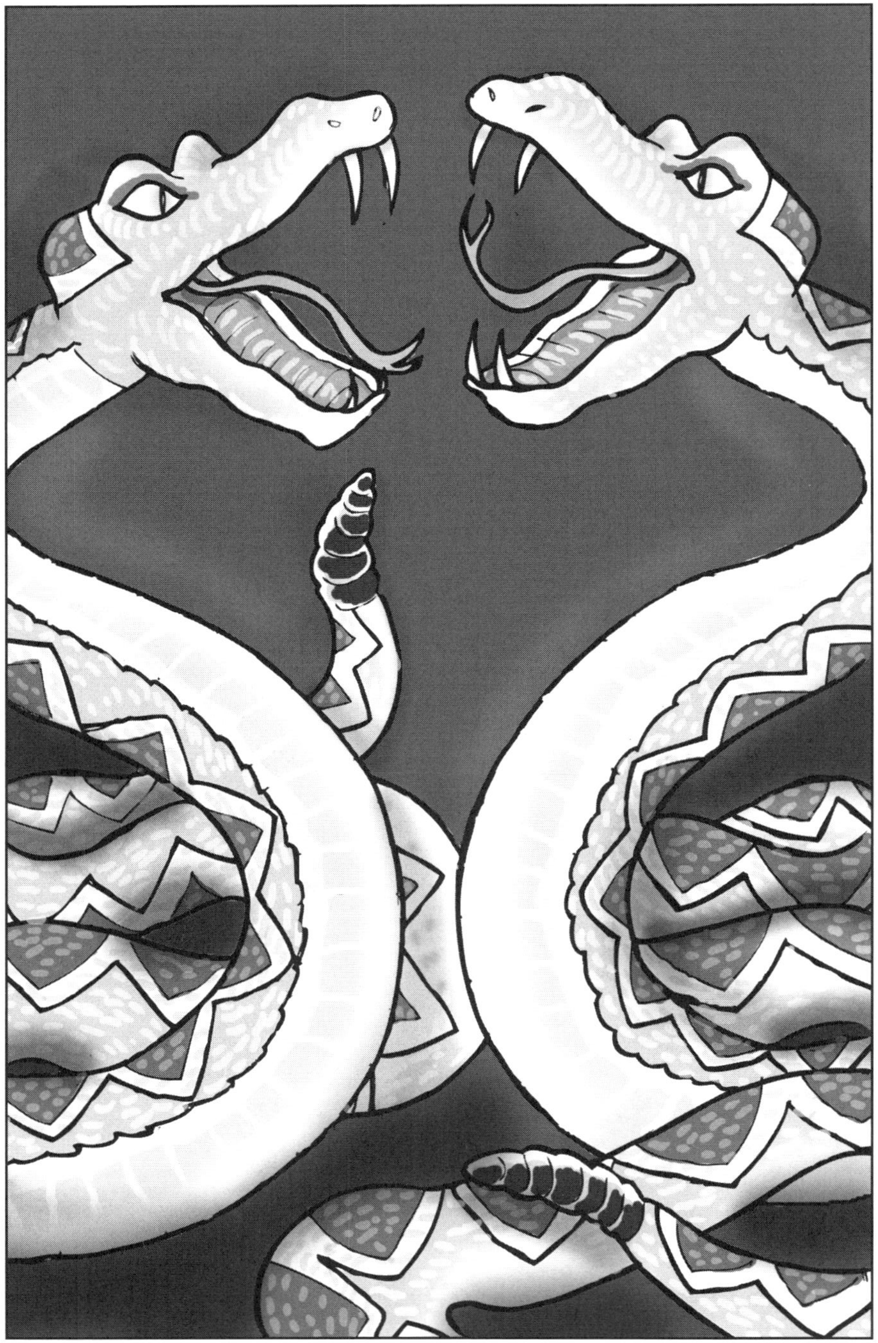

(Page 62)

Which are the scariest snakes with venom? I'd say the king cobra and the black mamba. The king cobra can grow 18 feet (5.5 m) long. It can rear up to look a 6 foot (1.8 m) man in the eye. The king cobra mostly eats other snakes. Still, its venom can kill an elephant in three hours.

The black mamba is quick to attack. And, its venom is the most deadly.

Scary! But don't forget. To a snake, you're a waste of venom!

It Slithers— Snakes

It's not easy being a snake. How do they catch food? They have no arms or legs. How do they fight other animals?

Most snakes use their jaws. There are about 2,700 types of snakes. Of those, 450 have a secret weapon. Not only can they bite — they can poison you!

Some snakes can fold up their fangs in their mouths. A Gaboon viper's fangs can measure up to two inches (5 cm) long. You would not want those fangs to sink into your leg!

Some snakes can control each fang on its own. They might only need to use one fang to get the job done. This also saves venom.

Of all the snakes, vipers have the most venom. Most of the viper's head is taken up with venom glands.

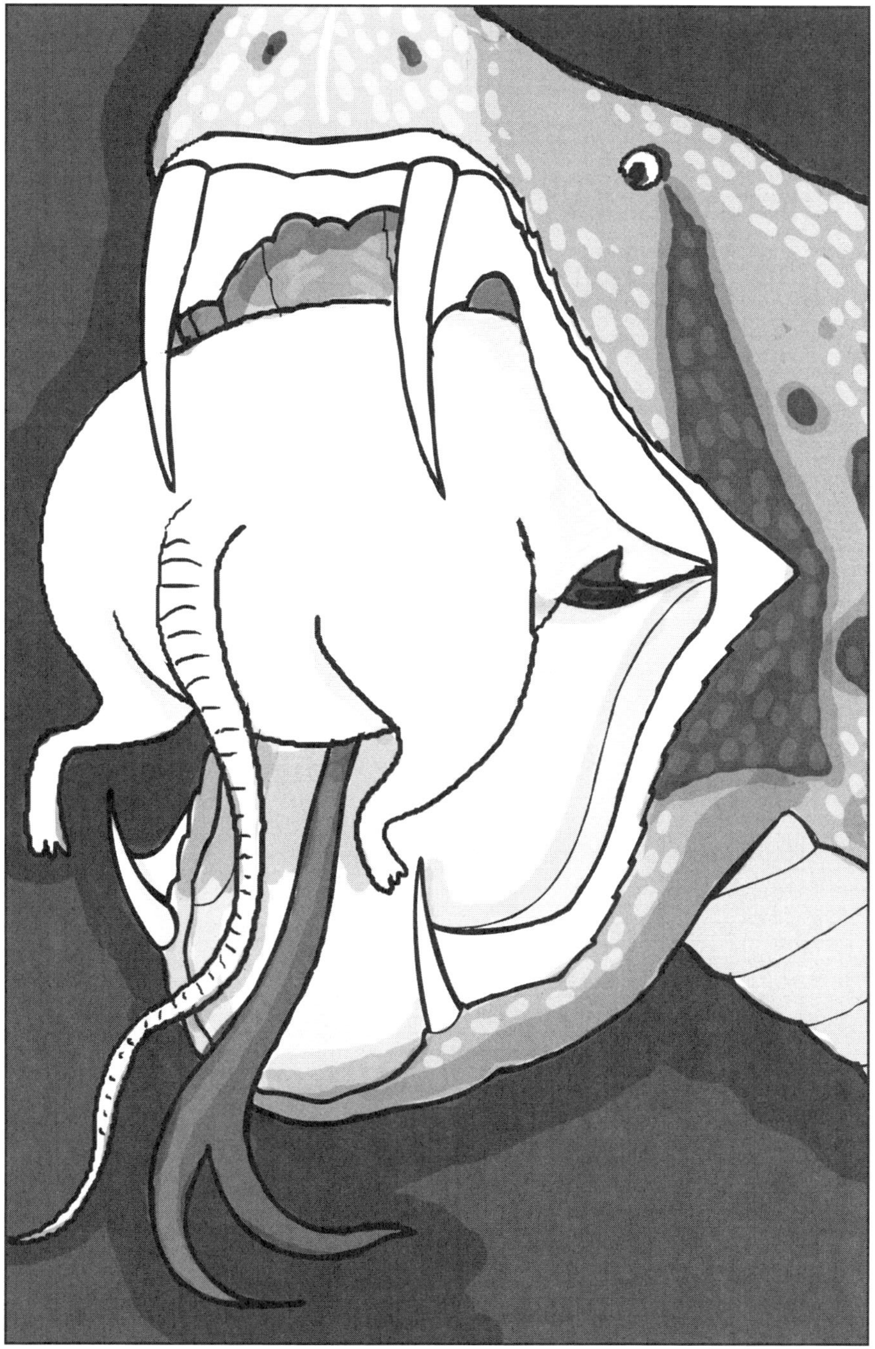

Most snakes do not use venom to kill. They use it to slow down their prey. A snake must not waste its venom. This is good news. A snake does not want to bite you. Getting food is the most important thing. It takes energy to make venom. And, it takes up to three weeks to refill.

So, snakes do other things to get out of trouble. Some snakes rattle. Some snakes can change their color. Some snakes give a dry bite. A dry bite has no venom. Over half of all rattlesnake bites are dry ones.

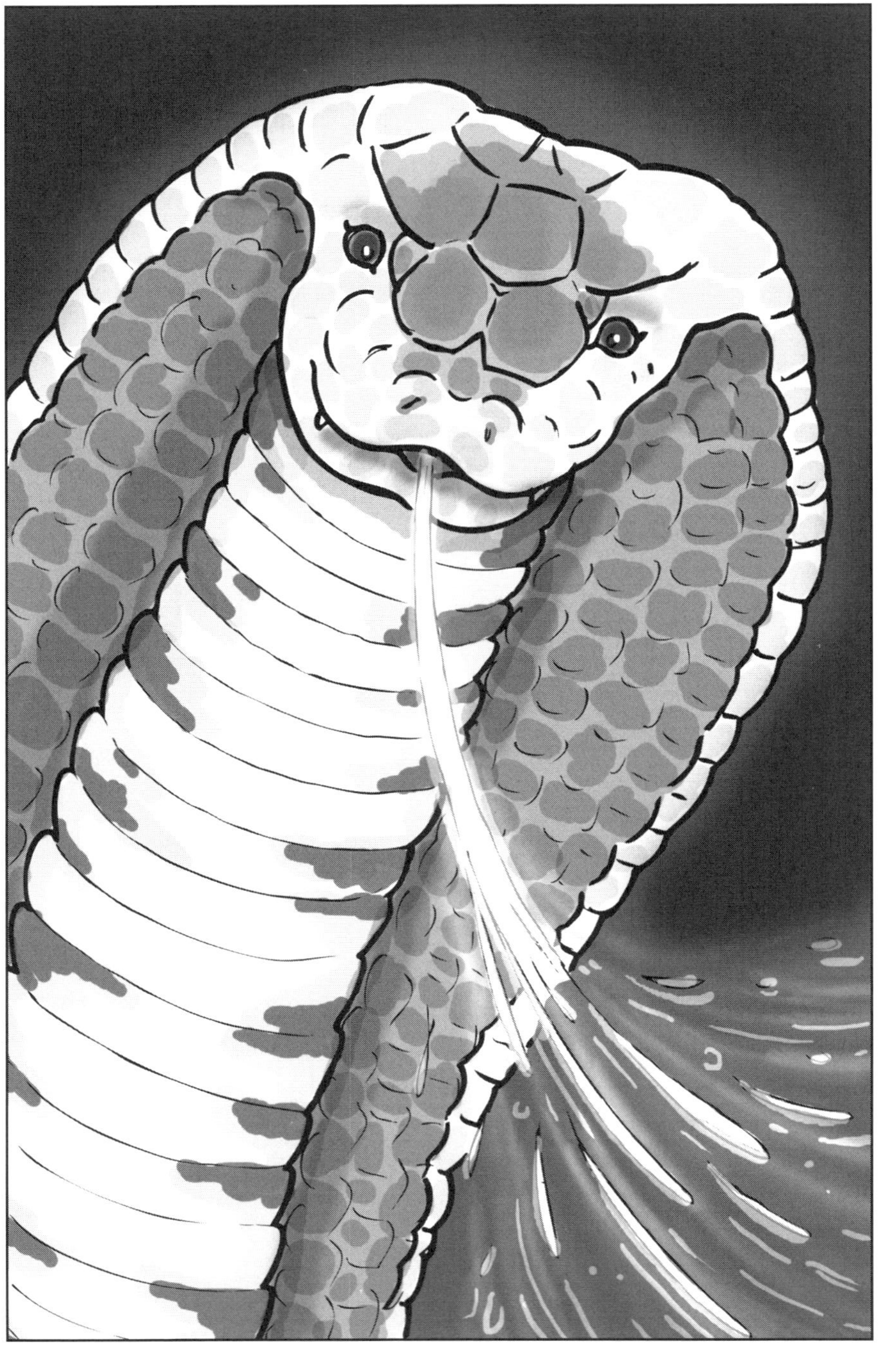

Snakes with no venom are more likely to bite. They have nothing to lose! It might hurt, but it won't kill you.

Spitting cobras can spit their venom. Other snakes shoot it from their mouths. Some snakes can spit eight feet (2.4 m)! Spitting doesn't kill. It can make the enemy blind for a while. This gives the snake time to escape — or attack. Spitters may spit 30 or 40 times and still give a fatal bite.

Name

Directions: Look at the picture and then make up your own story about it. *Creative Writing*

Name

Reading for details

Directions: Read each question. Circle the correct answer.

1. How many kinds of snakes are there in the world?

about 2,000 kinds of snakes

about 2,300 kinds of snakes

about 2,700 kinds of snakes

2. How many kinds of snakes have venom?

450 kinds of snakes have venom

550 kinds of snakes have venom

250 kinds of snakes have venom

3. Which kind of snake has the deadliest venom?

cobras

vipers

mambas

Draw a picture of a rattlesnake.	Write a sentence about a rattlesnake.
Draw a picture of a cobra.	Write a sentence about a cobra.

Fill in the blanks. Use the Word Bank.

Word Bank: birds dead eat feet handstand mouth opossum poop slime smell spray tastes

1. An opossum will foam at the _______________ to scare its enemies.
2. If foaming and snarling don't work, an opossom will play _______________.
3. The _______________ makes _______________ so that it smells like a dead animal.
4. A baby potato beetle _______________ very good to _______________.
5. A baby potato beetle covers itself in _______________ so that animals won't _______________ it.
6. Skunks use their bad _______________ to keep their enemies away.
7. Some skunks can shoot their _______________ ten feet (3 m).
8. A spotted skunk does a _______________ and waves its _______________ as a warning.

Let's draw a conclusion!

On another sheet of paper, answer this question. Animals have some clever ways to protect themselves. How would you protect yourself?

(Page 69)

Don't Mess with Me!

(Page 70)

Everyone knows about skunks. They use their gross smell to keep enemies away. But, you might not know how they do it. You might not want to know. I'm going to tell you anyway.

A skunk has two glands under its tail. The glands make the stinky spray. The spray shoots out of two nozzles. The skunk can even aim the spray. It can shoot the spray more than ten feet (3 m). If you get hit in the face you won't see for a while. And, you might throw up.

Spotted skunks warn you before they spray. They do a handstand and wave their back feet. If you see a skunk doing a handstand — don't clap. Run!

(Page 71)

Don't Mess with Me!

Animals have to take care of themselves. Every day is a fight to survive. Animals in the wild have two worries. First, they have to find their own food. Second, they have to stop from being food for someone else!

(Page 72)

A baby potato beetle does not put on a big show like the opossum. But it has to do something to stay safe. It doesn't have a hard shell until it's an adult. This makes it very tasty to birds.

So, the poor baby potato beetle does what it can. It uses its secret weapon. Sorry, it's poop again. The larva makes itself less tasty by covering itself in its own poop. What's more, the poop is toxic.

(Page 73)

It's not easy. Some animals have some weird ways to do this!

Have you ever been so scared you can't move? If the opossum is in danger, it snarls. If that doesn't work, it plays dead. It flops on its side. It foams at the mouth. It hangs its tongue out of its mouth. It pulls its lips back. It bares its teeth.

(Page 74)

Now, here comes the gross part. It poops on itself. And, (another gross part), it makes green slime. It smells like rotting skin. Most animals won't eat something that's already dead.

You can poke the opossum. You can turn it over. You can even carry it away. It just won't move.

You can see why this works. I wouldn't go near one. Would you? Opossums are good actors—but, not really. Experts say they don't try to do it. It just happens when they are scared. It's like fainting.

Name

Inference

Directions: Look at each picture. Write a sentence next to each picture about what you think is happening.

Name

Drawing Conclusions

Directions: Read the question in each box. Write your answer in each speech bubble.

1. What do you think the frog is thinking?	2. What do you think the skunk is thinking?

Fact or Opinion

Directions: A **fact** is something that is true. An **opinion** is something that a person thinks, believes, or feels. Write the word "**fact**" or the word "**opinion**" next to each sentence.

________________ 1. An opossum will play dead when it is scared.

________________ 2. Opossums look funny when they are upset.

________________ 3. Opossums smell bad when they make green slime.

________________ 4. A baby potato beetle puts on a big show to stay safe.

________________ 5. Everyone knows a lot about skunks.

________________ 6. Spotted skunks warn you before they spray.

Fill in the blanks. Use the Word Bank.

Word Bank: animal behind fast largest lion malaria mosquito prey scare spin tails world

1. Crocodiles catch their ________ and ________ it around.
2. An African ________ is one of the ________ of all the big cats.
3. Tigers attack from ________.
4. Scorpions are found all over the ________.
5. Scorpions use their ________ to pump out venom.
6. Moving ________ will ________ a snake.
7. The ________ is the number one most dangerous ________.
8. A disease called ________ comes from mosquitoes.

Let's draw a conclusion!

On another sheet of paper write a short story about another animal that you think is dangerous.

(Page 77)

The Most Dangerous Animals

(Page 78)

Number 1: Mosquitoes

Mosquitoes are the most dangerous creatures on the planet. Over one million people die each year from their bites.

Most people don't know they have been bitten right away. After the bites, red, itchy bumps come and can last for days.

Why are their bites so deadly? Mosquito saliva gets in the blood. The saliva carries a disease. It's called malaria. Many children in poor countries die of malaria. If more people had mosquito nets this would not happen as much. A lot of charities buy mosquito nets for people who can't afford them.

Tips: If you are in a country with malaria use a mosquito net. Your doctor will also give you pills. You must take them before, during, and after your visit.

(Page 79)

The Most Dangerous Animals

What are the most dangerous animals? I bet you can't guess. Here are the top five. Number one is the most deadly. There are also tips on how to get away from these animals! Let's hope you won't need to use the tips.

Number 5: Crocodiles

Crocodiles are fast. They come out of the water like rockets. They catch their prey and spin it around. It's hard to get away when you're dizzy!

Tip: Do not swim near crocodiles!

Number 2: Snakes

There are more than 2,700 kinds of snakes. Of those, 450 of them have venom. Only about 250 can kill. Snakes are fast. Any part of the human body is a good place to bite. The venom can get into a person's blood very fast.

Tips: Snakes attack if they are scared. So, stay away! If you come across a snake, back away very slowly. Moving fast will scare it.

(Page 81)

Number 4: Big Cats

The African lion is one the largest of the big cats. They often attack from above. They leap down from a tree or a rock. Tigers attack from behind.

Tips: Stare them in the eye. Don't look away. Don't turn and run. They are faster than you! Shout, scream, and throw stones. If one gets hold of you, punch its nose and eyes. Let's really hope you never need to use these tips.

Number 3: Scorpions

Scorpions are found all over the world. There are 1,400 types of scorpions. Only 25 of them are deadly.

Scorpions pump venom through the ends of their tails. The African spitting scorpion can spray venom over three feet (one meter).

Tips: Scorpions are busy at night. When camping, shake out any bedding and clothes. Wear thick socks. Or, stay in a hotel!

Name

Directions: Think about the story you have read.
Draw a line from the sentence to its matching picture.

1. Snakes attack if they are scared.

2. If you are in a country with malaria use a mosquito net.

3. Crocodiles come out of the water like rockets.

4. Scorpions are found all over the world.

5. The African lion often attacks from above, and tigers attack from behind.

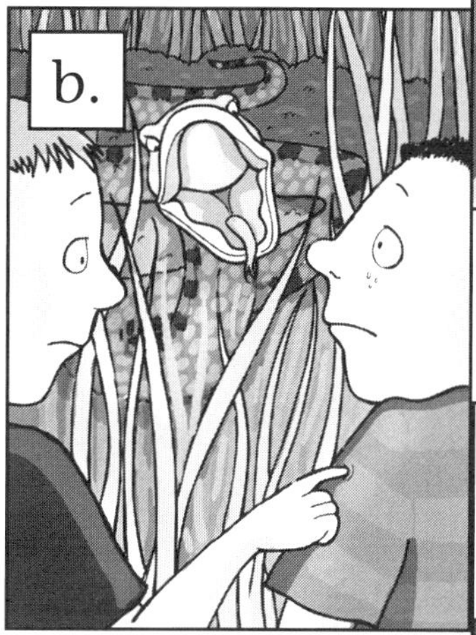

Name

Directions: **Antonyms** are two different words that have the opposite meaning. For example, "hot" and "cold" are antonyms. Draw a line from each word in **Column A** to its matching antonym in **Column B**.

Column A	Column B
up	**healthy**
mean	**little**
dangerous	**down**
sick	**quiet**
loud	**nice**
big	**safe**

Directions: Write an answer to the following question.

What would you do if you came upon a venomous snake?

Fill in the blanks. Use the Word Bank.

Word Bank: 20 30 college computer hands microwave monkeys old six south ten trained work

1. Capuchin _______________ are being _______________ to help people.
2. Monkeys are good with their _______________.
3. Capuchin monkeys come from _______________ America.
4. They only weigh between _______________ and _______________ pounds.
5. These monkeys go to Monkey _______________.
6. The monkeys learn how to turn on a _______________ and _______________.
7. Caphuchin monkeys live for _______________ to _______________ years.
8. Helping Hands even looks after the monkeys who are too _______________ to _______________.

Let's draw a conclusion!

On another sheet of paper, make a list of all the things that you think a capuchin monkey could learn to do.

(Page 85)

Nonfiction—Story 11

Then, the monkey and owner start their new life. Helping Hands often checks that the monkey and the owner are well and happy. Capuchin monkeys can live to be 20 to 30 years old. Helping Hands makes sure the monkeys are looked after—even when the monkeys get too old to work.

Craig Cook has a capuchin monkey from Helping Hands. He doesn't know how he lived before Minnie came to be with him.

"Minnie and I share a bond I never knew I could ever have," says Craig. "We're a pretty awesome team together."

(Page 87)

Helping Hands—Capuchin Monkeys

We all know about "seeing eye" or "guide" dogs. These dogs are trained to help people with disabilities. They help their owners to be more free. People can go out, cross a busy street, and go to the store. Plus, guide dogs make great friends.

You may not know about "Helping Hands" monkeys. These are capuchin monkeys. They help people who can't move from the neck down. A charity, called Helping Hands, was sure that monkeys could help people. Monkeys are clever. They are curious. They like to play. They are good with their hands.

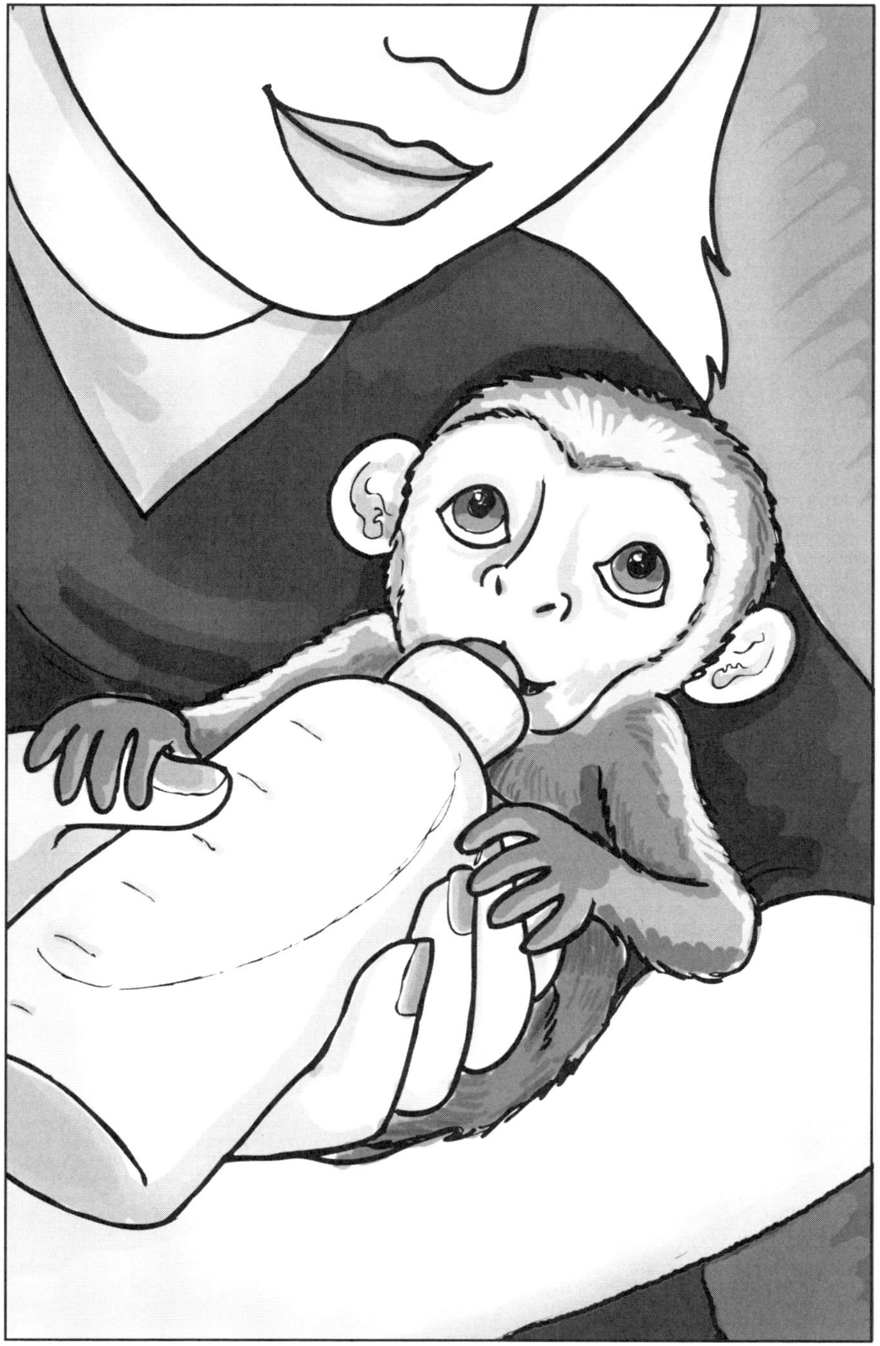

(Page 88)

The monkey is still not ready to start work yet. The owner may need some special jobs done. While still at Monkey College, the monkey learns how to do these special jobs.

Finally, the monkey is ready for its new home. At first, the trainer will go too. She spends time in the home with the monkey. She makes sure the monkey knows exactly what to do.

(Page 89)

Capuchin monkeys come from South America. They only weigh six to ten pounds (2.7 to 4.5 kg). In the wild, these monkeys use tools with their hands. They are quite easy to train. They also like people — which is very important!

So, Helping Hands now breeds capuchins in a Boston zoo. At first, the young monkeys live with trained caregivers. When they are older, they go to Monkey College.

At Monkey College they learn how to do basic jobs. Things that can help any disabled person. How to turn on a radio. Open a jar. Turn on a microwave. Take things in and out of the refrigerator. Pick up the phone. Turn on the computer.

The charity gets to know each monkey well. They know what it can do. They know what it likes to do and what it is good at. The next stage is to choose someone the monkey will get along with.

Name

Directions: Choose a word from the Word Bank to answer each crossword question. Write the answer in the correct word boxes.

Word Bank capuchin Boston dogs friends on out radios

ACROSS

4. __________ monkeys can learn many jobs.
5. Capuchin monkeys can turn ________ computers.
6. Guide ______ also help people.
7. Capuchin monkeys are born at a zoo in ________ .

DOWN

1. Capuchin monkeys and people can become good _______.
2. Capuchin monkeys can turn on _______.
3. These monkeys can take food _______ of the refrigerator

Name

Directions: Write an answer to the following question. *Drawing Conclusions*

Pretend you are a foster parent to a capuchin monkey.
What are some of the things you would do with your baby monkey?

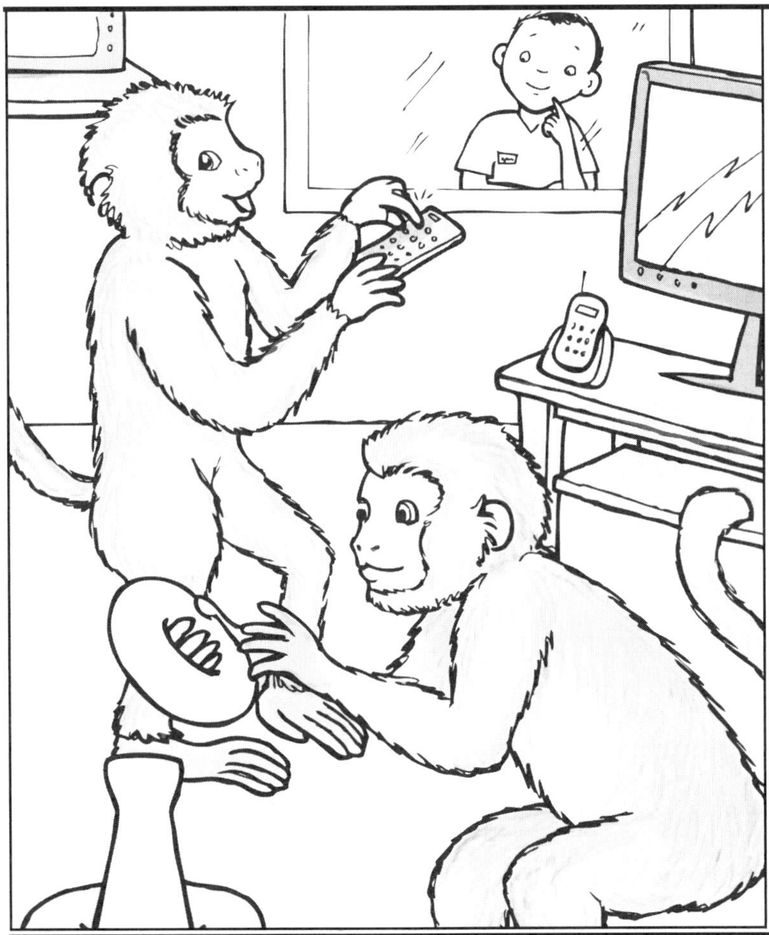

Following Directions

Directions: Here is a picture from the story. Follow the directions.

1. Color one monkey gray.
2. Color the other monkey brown.
3. Color the boy's shirt red.
4. Circle the two remote controls.
5. Draw a line under the window.
6. Draw glasses on the boy.
7. Color the TV screen black.

Fill in the blanks. Use the Word Bank.

Word Bank:	blanket	brave	dogs	Endal
help knocked	medals	Orca	slope	World

1. Maria Dickin had an idea that ____________ could be given to ______________ animals.
2. During ______________ War II, 54 medals were awarded to animals.
3. Since 2002, all the PDSA Gold Medals have gone to ______________.
4. One day, Allen was ______________ out of his wheelchair.
5. Allen's dog, ______________, pulled a ______________ from the car.
6. Endal ran to get ______________.
7. Cheryl Smith had a dog named ____________.
8. Cheryl fell down a ______________, and Orca ran to run get help.

Let's draw a conclusion!

On another sheet of paper, write a short story about a "furry hero." What did the animal do to earn the title "hero"?

(Page 93)

Furry Heroes

(Page 94)

Orca ran to the first person he saw. The man thought Orca was lost. He took Orca's collar and tried to walk him home. Orca broke free and ran on.

Then, Orca found Cheryl's neighbor who was out jogging. He knew that Orca was trying to say something. Orca led the neighbor to Cheryl. The neighbor called for help. Orca stayed at Cheryl's side.

These two dogs are amazing life-saving pets!

(Page 95)

Furry Heroes

Heroes come in all shapes and sizes. In 1943, a woman called Maria Dickin had an idea for a medal. It was for animals who had been brave in a war.

During World War II, Maria Dickin's charity gave 54 medals to animals —32 pigeons, 18 dogs, 3 horses, and 1 cat.

In May 2003, Cheryl Smith was a student. She was out in her wheelchair. As always, her dog Orca ran next to her. Suddenly, the wheelchair hit a rock on the path. Cheryl fell out of the chair and down a 15-foot slope (4.6 m).

At the bottom of the slope was a ditch filled with water. Cheryl was in the cold water. The wheelchair fell on top of her. Now, she couldn't move at all. Orca was trained not to leave Cheryl. Not until Cheryl said, "Get help!" did Orca go.

In 2001, the same charity started a new medal. It is called the PDSA* Gold Medal. It is given to very brave and very loyal animals. The medal has been given 18 times since 2001. So far, all the medals have been given to dogs. Here are two stories about two amazing dogs.

* ***Note:*** PDSA is a veterinary charity in the United Kingdom called "The People's Dispensary for Sick Animals." (PDSA)

Allen Parton was in a car crash in 1991. It left him unable to walk, speak, or write. Then, Endal came to live with Allen. The dog helped Allen face life again. They were very close.

One day, Allen and Endal were in a hotel car park. Allen was knocked out of his wheelchair. He was lying on the cold ground. Endal pulled a blanket from the car. He put it over Allen. Then, Endal waited. As soon as Allen came to, he ran to get help.

Name

Drawing Conclusions

Directions: Read the question in each box. Write your answer in each speech bubble.

1. What do you think the pigeon is thinking?

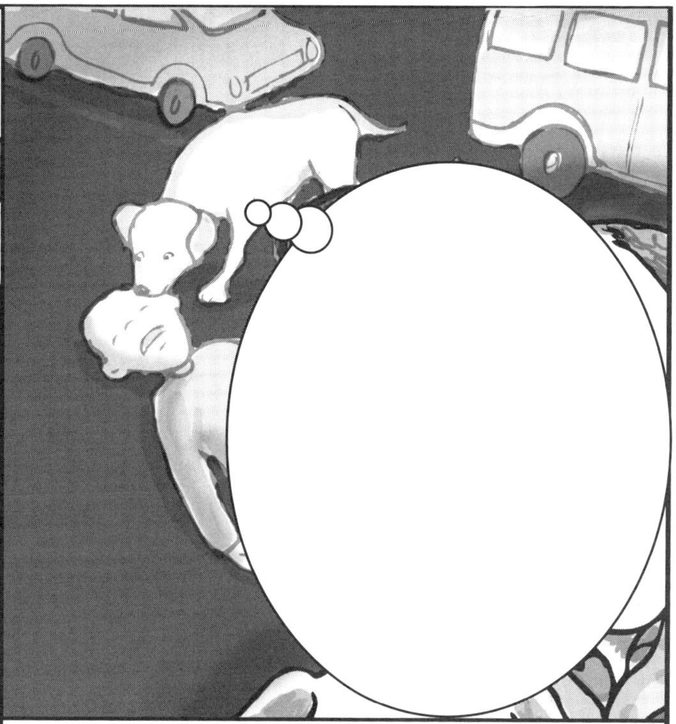

2. What do you think Endal is thinking?

3. What do you think Cheryl is saying to Orca?

4. What do you think Orca is thinking?

Name

Directions: Circle the words from the Word Bank in the word search. The words may be horizontal or vertical.

Word Search

Word Bank
brave
cats
collar
crash
dogs
helped
horses
loyal
medal
move
pigeons

d	h	q	m	o	v	e	w	h
p	i	g	e	o	n	s	h	o
c	l	u	d	t	i	r	r	r
o	o	c	a	t	s	o	d	s
l	y	r	l	b	r	a	v	e
l	a	a	r	o	d	o	g	s
a	l	s	n	t	n	y	e	z
r	l	h	e	l	p	e	d	r

Directions: Circle **yes** or **no** for each sentence.

Reading for Details

1. Maria Dickin had an idea for a bravery medal for animals. **yes** **no**

2. During World War II Maria Dickin's charity gave medals to 32 parrots and 17 dogs. **yes** **no**

3. In 2002, the Gold Medal has been given to 12 dogs and 9 cats. **yes** **no**

4. Endal belongs to Allen Parton. **yes** **no**

5. Orca belongs to Cheryl Smith. **yes** **no**

6. Endal and Orca are life-saving pets. **yes** **no**

Fill in the blanks. Use the Word Bank.

Word Bank: beaver dam door eat fix kits home leaves lodge plants pond sleep

1. A ________________ needs a ________________ to make a safe home.
2. If a ________________ breaks, the beavers will rush to ________________ it.
3. A beaver's ________________ is called a ________________.
4. A lodge is built with sticks, bark, rocks, mud, grass, ________________, and ________________.
5. Beavers build an underwater ________________.
6. Beavers ________________ on the first floor of their lodge.
7. Beavers ________________ on the second floor of their lodge.
8. Baby beavers are called ________________.

Let's draw a conclusion!

On another sheet of paper, draw a picture of a beaver. Include everything that is talked about on page 9. Label your picture.

(Page 101)

BEAVERS— CONSTRUCTION WORKERS

(Page 102)

Beavers are born ready for action. Baby beavers are called kits. When they are born, the kit's eyes are open. Half an hour later, they can swim! After a month, they can hold their breath and swim underwater.

Beavers have mates for life. A mother beaver looks after babies and teenagers at the same time. Teenage beavers help with the new babies.

What amazing animals!

(Page 103)

BEAVERS— CONSTRUCTION WORKERS

No other animals can do what beavers do. They change where they live. They choose a spot and build a dam. This floods the area and makes a pond. Beavers need a pond to make their home safe.

The longest beaver dam on record is 2,790 feet (850 m) long! It took over 20 years to build and has two lodges. It is in Alberta, Canada.

(Page 104)

Beavers are clever animals with clever bodies. Their large, webbed feet are like fins. Their ears and nostrils have valves. These close when they are underwater. Fur lined lips form a seal behind their teeth. This lets them hold their breath while still using their teeth underwater.

Coolest of all, they have a set of see-through eyelids — built-in goggles! Beavers can stay underwater for 15 minutes. Their flat tails help them sit and stand. In water, their tails help them steer. When there is danger, they slap the water with their tails.

(Page 105)

If a dam breaks, the beavers rush around to fix it. If they are not fast, they could lose all the water in their pond.

Once the pond is deep, the beavers begin to build their lodge. They do this with sticks, bark, rocks, mud, grass, leaves, and plants. When it is built, the beavers swim under the water. They dig or chew a tunnel door. This underwater door stops guests they don't want!

The first floor is a few inches above the water level. In here the beavers eat and dry off. On the second floor they sleep and care for the babies. Beavers shred wood and plants to make a carpet for the floor.

A lodge is home for up to 18 beavers. In the winter, beavers stay in their cozy lodges.

Name

Directions: This is a picture of a beaver's lodge.
Follow the directions.

FOLLOW THE DIRECTIONS

1. Color the sky blue.
2. Color all of the beavers brown.
3. Color the water light blue.
4. Color the outside of the lodge brown.
5. Color the grass green.
6. Circle the two beavers that are swimming underwater.
7. Draw a line under the two baby beavers.
8. Draw an "X" next to the beaver on the grassy hill.
9. Draw a "T" next to the beaver standing on top of the lodge.
10. Draw a sun in the sky and color it yellow.
11. Draw and color another beaver swimming in the water.

Name

Directions: A **fact** is something that is true. An **opinion** is something that a person thinks, believes, or feels. Write the word "**fact**" or the word "**opinion**" next to each sentence.

__________ 1. Beavers need ponds to make their homes safe.

__________ 2. The longest beaver dam on record is 2,790 feet long.

__________ 3. Beavers have a lot of fun chopping down trees.

__________ 4. A beaver lodge has an underwater tunnel door.

__________ 5. Beavers believe their homes are safer than other animals' home.

__________ 6. Beavers have see-through eyelids.

Directions: You have learned a lot after reading *Beavers–Construction Workers.* What are some other things that you would like to know about beavers?

What I want to know!

Fill in the blanks. Use the Word Bank.

Word Bank: ate days dog escalator George jumped most mouth pig tallest TV watched

(Page 109)

1. Bibby held 10 rattlesnakes in his ____________.
2. Ken Edwards ________________ 36 cockroaches on live ________________.
3. A pot-bellied ________________ from Japan ________________ higher than any other pig.
4. The smallest ________________ is called Heaven Sent Brandy.
5. The ________________ dog is a Great Dane named Giant ________________.
6. A man from Sri Lanka ________________ TV on a sofa for 72 hours.
7. This same man also rode an ________________ for five ________________.
8. Ashrita Furman holds the ________________ World Records.

Let's draw a conclusion!

On another sheet of paper, answer this question. If you could set a crazy world record, what would you do?

Nonfiction—Story 14

(Page 110)

Ashrita Furman holds the most World Records. When we wrote this book he held over 100 records. These are just a few:

- Walked with a milk bottle on his head for 80.96 miles (130.3 km).
- Most Hop-Scotch Games in 24 Hours—434.
- Most Rope Jumps in 24 Hours—130,000.
- Fastest 6.2 mile (10 km) Sack Race —1 hour 25 minutes 10 seconds.
- Most Underwater Rope Jumps in One Hour—738.
- Fastest Pogo Stick Climb of Canada's CN Tower—57 minutes 51 seconds.

What's your record going to be?

(Page 111)

Crazy World records

Ever wanted to set a world record? It's hard to come up with a new one. There are lots out there!

You might need to be brave. Jackie Bibby held 10 rattlesnakes in his mouth. He held them by their tails for 10 seconds. He also sat in a bathtub with 87 snakes. Clint Ewing rode through a tunnel of fire on his motorbike. Karoline Mariechen Meyer held her breath underwater for 18 minutes, 32.59 seconds.

(Page 112)

Some people like to hold lots of records. Suresh Joachim from Sri Lanka does. Here are some of them:

He watched TV on the sofa for over 69 hours. He rode an escalator for 5 days. He crawled over 35 miles (56.6 km). He rocked in a rocking chair for 75 hours. He ironed 639 pieces of clothing in 55 hours.

(Page 113)

Or, you could set gross records. Ken Edwards ate 36 cockroaches in one minute on live television. He also put 47 rats down his pants.

Are you strong? John Evans put a car on his head for 33 seconds. How do you think he got a car on his head?

Or, are you just plain silly? The longest chain of underwear was made in Cyprus. Niek Vermeulen collected 5,468 air sickness bags. (Let's hope they were not used!)

Animals hold records too. Kotetsu is a pot-bellied pig from Japan. He jumped higher than any other pig at over 2 feet (70 cm). Cinderella May holds the record for the dog high jump—5 feet, 8 inches (172.7 cm).

The smallest dog is called Heaven Sent Brandy. From her nose to the tip of her tail, the Chihuahua was 6 inches (15.2 cm) long. The tallest dog living is Giant George, a Great Dane. He is over 7 feet (2.2 m) long.

Augie is a golden retriever from Texas. He picked up and held five tennis balls in his mouth. (It's not just humans that hold silly records!)

Name

Directions: These are animals who have set world records: the highest-jumping pig, the tallest dog, and the smallest dog. Follow the directions.

FOLLOW THE DIRECTIONS

1. Color the pig black.
2. Color the pig's skirt pink.
3. Color the Great Dane dark brown.
4. Color the Great Dane's collar yellow.
5. Color the Chihuahua light brown.
6. Color the Chihuahua's stool blue and green.
7. Color the background red.
8. Draw an "X" next to the pig.
9. Draw a line under the Chihuahua.
10. Draw a circle around the letter "G."
11. Print each animal's name on the the back of this paper.

Name

Main Idea

Directions: The **main idea** tells what the story is about. Read the following sentences and circle the sentence that you think best explains the main idea of the story.

1. Animals have set some of the craziest world records.

2. Anyone can set a crazy world record.

3. There are many strange and crazy world records.

Antonyms

Directions: **Antonyms** are two different words that have the opposite meaning. For example, "hot" and "cold" are antonyms. Draw a line from each word in **Column A** to its matching antonym in **Column B**.

Column A	Column B
tallest	**dirty**
serious	**slow**
strong	**shortest**
fast	**water**
fire	**silly**
clean	**weak**

(Page 117)

MY OWN STORY

(Page 118)

(Page 119)

(Page 121)

(Page 122)

New Vocabulary to Be Introduced Prior to Reading Each Story

Story 1: Animals—Beauty or Beast?
- Aye-aye
- beast
- beauty
- bushy
- cuddle
- greasy
- oily
- Sphynx cat

Story 2: Dolphins—What's Not to Like?
- dangerous
- dolphins
- experts
- filter
- hemisphere
- humans
- humpback
- marine
- trainer

Story 3: The World's Most Disgusting Animal
- Asia
- disgusting
- gallons
- hagfish
- nostril
- oozes
- pores
- slime
- squeezes
- tongue

Story 4: Don't Let the Bed Bugs Bite
- clutter
- environment
- insecticide
- mattresses
- mosquitoes
- vacuum cleaners

Story 5: The Monster in the Aquarium
- aquarium
- attacked
- bristles
- coral
- disaster
- display
- England
- reef
- stomachs
- thousands

Story 6: Purse Dogs
- Bichon Frises
- bladder
- breeds
- Britney Spears
- Bruiser
- Chihuahuas
- fashion
- Harvard
- important
- Jessica Simpson
- Maltese
- Paris Hilton
- Pomeranians
- Roman
- teacup poodles
- weigh
- Yorkshire terrier

Story 7: The Weirdest Dinosaurs
- Antarctica
- coolest
- crest
- Cryolophosaurus
- dinosaur
- Elvisaurus
- reptile
- Tanystropheus
- Therizinosaurus
- weirdest

Story 8: It Slithers—Snakes
- energy
- Gaboon viper
- glands
- mamba
- measure
- poison
- prey
- rattlesnake
- scariest
- spitting cobras
- venom
- weapon

Story 9: Don't Mess with Me!
- actors
- handstand
- fainting
- nozzles
- opossum
- potato beetle
- rotting
- skunks
- survive
- toxic

Story 10: The Most Dangerous Animals
- African
- creatures
- crocodiles
- dangerous
- malaria
- mosquito
- saliva
- scorpion
- venom

Story 11: Helping Hands—Capuchin Monkeys
- awesome
- Boston
- breeds
- capuchin
- charity
- college
- computer
- curious
- disabilities
- microwaves
- refrigerator
- South America
- special
- trainer

Story 12: Furry Heroes
- Allen Parton
- amazing
- Cheryl Smith
- collar
- ditch
- Endal
- knocked
- loyal
- Maria Dickin
- medals
- neighbor
- Orca
- pigeon
- slope
- wheelchair

Story 13: Beavers—Construction Workers
- beaver
- construction
- cozy
- dam
- lodge
- nostrils
- shred
- tunnel
- underwater
- valves

Story 14: Crazy World Records
- Ashrita Furman
- Augie
- Canada's
- Chihuahua
- Clint Ewing
- cockroaches
- Cyprus
- escalator
- golden retriever
- Heaven Sent Brandy
- Jackie Bibby
- Japan
- John Evans
- Karoline Mariechen Meyer
- Ken Edwards
- Kotetsu
- motorbike
- Niek Vermeulen
- rattlesnakes
- Sri Lanka
- Suresh Joachim
- Texas

Answer Key

Story 1
Animals—Beauty or Beast?

Booklet page 12 (page 5):

1. cat, hair
2. skin
3. cold
4. sleep, warm
5. aye-ayes
6. long, tails
7. stop
8. bugs

Page 11

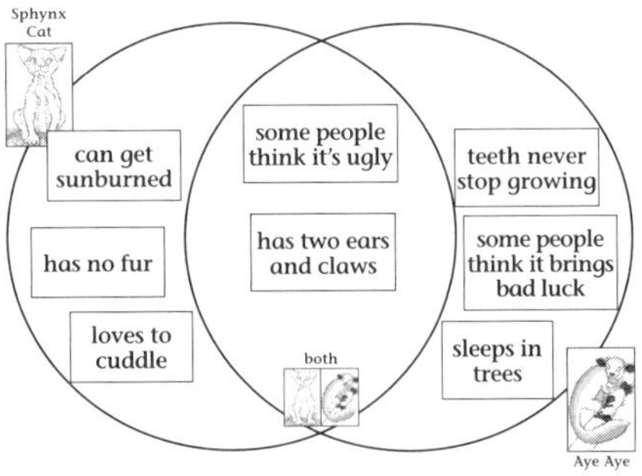

Page 12 (Top)

b	e	a	u	t	y	n	t	a
e	n	t	g	o	n	c	t	y
a	k	h	l	j	e	l	a	e
s	p	h	y	n	x	a	i	a
t	e	r	o	e	i	w	l	y
c	t	s	s	e	o	s	s	e
v	s	m	s	l	e	e	p	j
a	n	i	m	a	l	s	l	a

Page 12 (Bottom)

1. T, 2. F, 3. T, 4. F, 5. T, 6. F

Story 2
Dolphins—
What's Not to Like?

Booklet page 12 (page 13):

1. Dolphins
2. sharks
3. play, animals
4. flick
5. brain, humans
6. trained, trash
7. fish
8. hid

Page 19

Check students' work

Page 20 (Top)

1. c., 2. a., 3. d., 4. b.

Page 20 (Bottom)

Check students' work

Story 3
The World's Most
Disgusting Animal

Booklet page 12 (page 21):

1. worm, eel
2. one
3. no
4. tongue, teeth
5. dead, eats
6. slime
7. ties
8. clean

Page 27

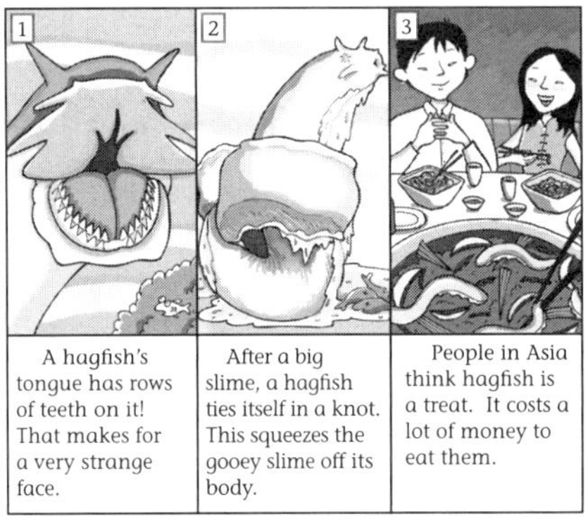

Page 28 (Top)

Check students' work

Page 28 (Bottom)

1. yes, 2. no, 3. yes, 4. yes, 5. no, 6. yes, 7. no

Story 4
Don't Let
the Bed Bugs Bite

Booklet page 12 (page 29):

1. bed bugs
2. sting
3. hurt, itch
4. eat, year
5. red, body
6. apple seed
7. hide
8. heat, cold

Page 35

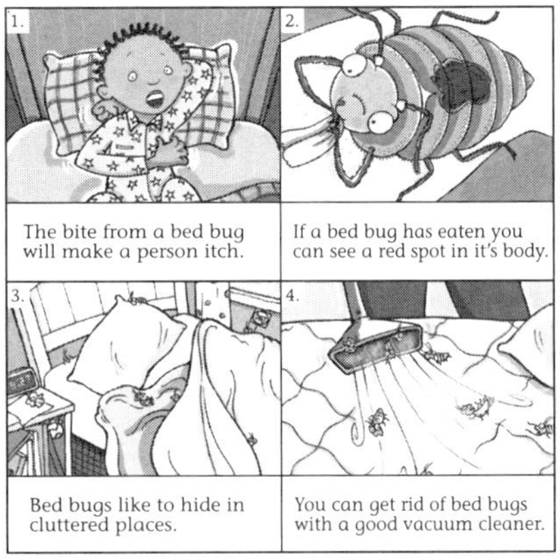

Page 36 (Top)

Check students' work

Page 36 (Bottom)

3. Learn all about bed bugs—where they live, what they eat, and how to get rid of them.

Story 5
The Monster
in the Aquarium

Booklet page 12 (page 37):

1. England
2. coral
3. giant reef worm
4. four
5. jaws, bristles
6. numb
7. caught, tank
8. Barry

Page 43

Check students' work

Page 44 (Top)

Check students' work

Page 44 (Bottom)

1. d., 2. a., 3. b., 4. c.

Story 6
Purse Dogs

Booklet page 12 (page 45):

1. Bruiser, dogs
2. buy
3. necklaces, beds
4. less, five
5. small, purse
6. bladder
7. washed
8. sleeves

Page 51

Page 52 (Top)

1. a. Bruiser, 2. b. Tinkerbell, 3. c. 5 pounds, 4. b. sleeves

Page 52 (Bottom)

Check students' work

Story 7
The Weirdest Dinosaurs

Booklet page 12 (page 53):

1. feet
2. Antarctica
3. crest, chicken
4. neck, ten
5. fishing
6. claws, three
7. not
8. food

Page 59

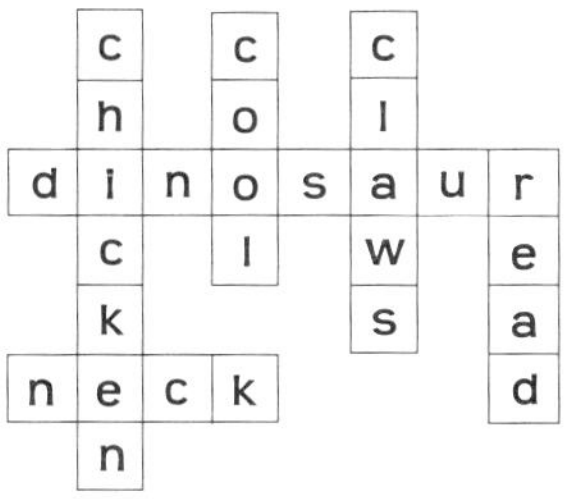

Page 60 (Top)

Check students' work

Page 60 (Bottom)

1. T, 2. T, 3. F, 4. T, 5. F, 6. T

Story 8
It Slithers—Snakes

Booklet page 12 (page 61):

1. fight
2. snakes, venom
3. energy
4. rattle
5. color
6. spit, eight
7. fangs
8. feet

Page 67

Check students' work

Page 68 (Top)

1. 2700 kinds of snakes
2. 450 kinds of snakes have venom
3. mambas

Page 68 (Bottom)

Check students' work

Story 9
Don't Mess with Me!

Booklet page 12 (page 69):

1. mouth
2. dead
3. opossum, slime
4. tastes, birds
5. poop, eat
6. smell
7. spray
8. handstand, feet

Page 75

Check students' work

Page 76 (Top)

Check students' work

Page 76 (Bottom)

1. fact, 2. opinion, 3. fact, 4. opinion, 5. opinion, 6. fact

Story 10
The Most Dangerous Animals

Booklet page 12 (page 77):

1. prey, spin
2. lion, largest
3. behind
4. world
5. tails
6. fast, scare
7. mosquito, animal
8. malaria

Page 83

1. b, 2. d, 3. a, 4. e, 5. c

Page 84 (Top)

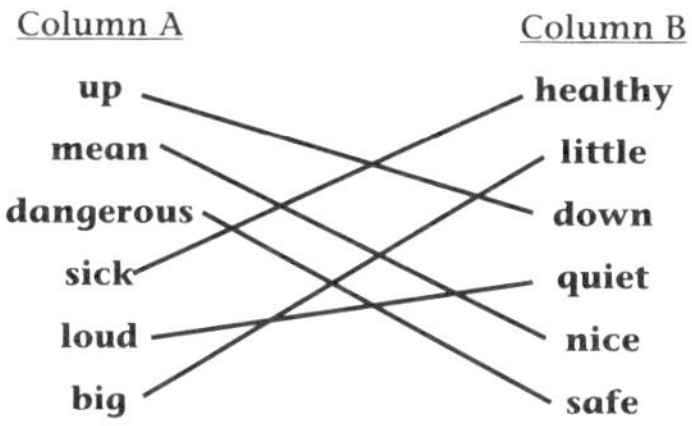

Page 84 (Bottom)

Check students' work

Story 11
Helping Hands—Capuchin Monkeys

Booklet page 12 (page 85):

1. monkeys, trained
2. hands
3. South
4. six, ten
5. College
6. microwave, computer
7. twenty, thirty
8. old, work

Page 91

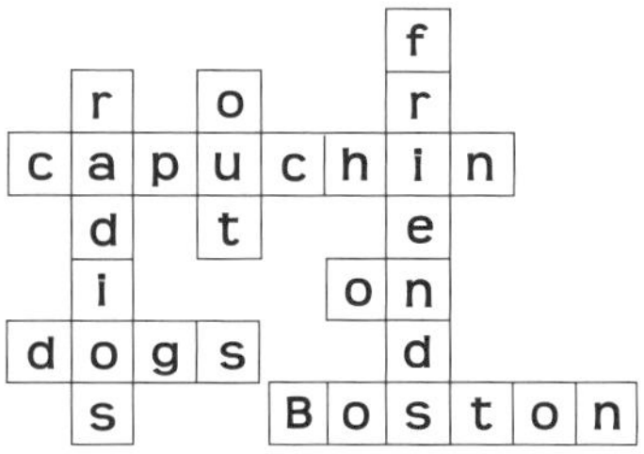

Page 92 (Top)
Check students' work

Page 92 (Bottom)
Check students' work

Story 12 – Furry Heroes

Booklet page 12 (page 93):
1. medals, brave
2. World
3. dogs
4. knocked
5. Endal, blanket
6. help
7. Orca
8. slope

Page 99
Check students' work

Page 100 (Top)

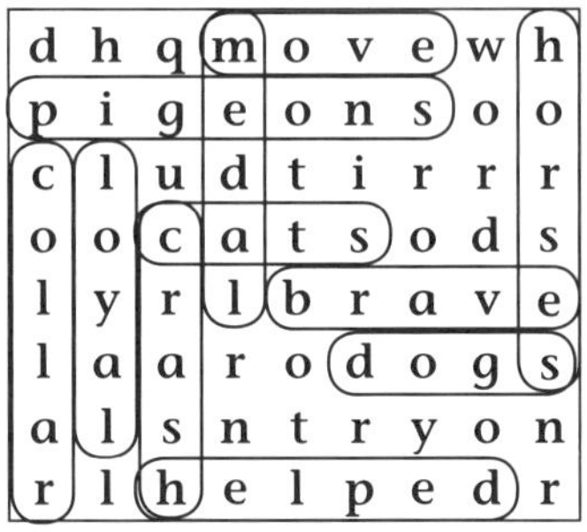

Page 100 (Bottom)
1. yes, 2. no, 3. no, 4. yes, 5. yes, 6. yes

Story 13 Beavers— Construction Workers

Booklet page 12 (page 101):
1. beaver, pond
2. dam, fix
3. home, lodge
4. leaves, plants
5. door
6. eat
7. sleep
8. kits

Page 107
Check students' work

Page 108 (Top)
1. fact, 2. fact, 3. opinion, 4. fact, 5. opinion, 6. fact

Page 108 (Bottom)
Check students' work

Story 14 Crazy World Records

Booklet page 12 (page 109):
1. mouth
2. ate, TV
3. pig, jumped
4. dog
5. tallest, George
6. watched
7. escalator, days
8. most

Page 115
Check students' work

Page 1116 (Top)
3. There are many strange and crazy world records.

Page 1117 (Bottom)

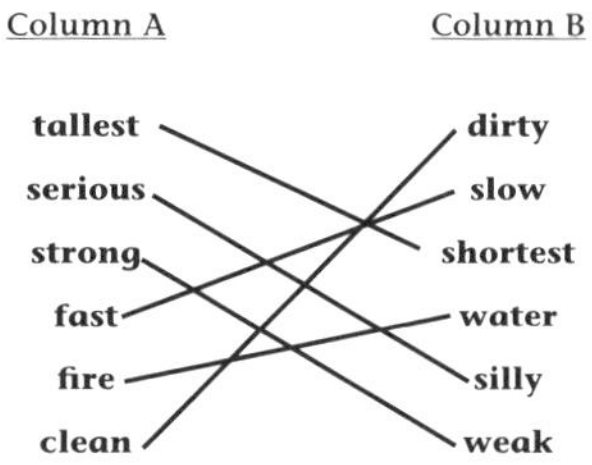

Correlations to the Standards

This book supports the NCTE/IRA *Standards for the English Language Arts.*

Each activity in this book supports one or more of the following standards:

1. **Students read many different types of print and nonprint texts for a variety of purposes.** *Trendy Topics: Nonfiction* includes 15 reading passages at varying reading levels, along with audio recordings of those passages to build both reading and listening skills. It also includes comprehension activities that require students to read and interpret images.

2. **Students use a variety of strategies to build meaning while reading.** Comprehension activities focusing on drawing conclusions, main idea, classification, cause and effect, reading for details, sequencing, inference, and vocabulary, among other skills, support this standard.

3. **Students communicate in spoken, written, and visual form, for a variety of purposes and a variety of audiences.** Activities in *Trendy Topics: Nonfiction* incorporate drawing and writing for a variety of purposes and audiences.

4. **Students use the writing process to write for different purposes and different audiences.** *Trendy Topics: Nonfiction* includes writing activities focused on a variety of audiences and purposes.

5. **Students incorporate knowledge of language conventions (grammar, spelling, punctuation), media techniques, and genre to create and discuss a variety of print and nonprint texts.** Writing activities in *Trendy Topics: Nonfiction* take different forms, such as sentences, lists, stories, and interview questions, allowing students to practice different forms of writing and writing conventions.

6. **Students use spoken, written, and visual language for their own purposes, such as to learn, for enjoyment, or to share information.** The engaging stories in *Trendy Topics: Nonfiction* will motivate students to read independently and the skill-building activities will support students in becoming more effective independent readers and writers.

How to Download the CD–Audio and PFD Files

To play the Audio stories in a CD Player

Place the CD in a CD player and play the CD as you would any audio or music CD. The pdf files on the CD will not appear or interfere with the audio stories.

Download the CD into a Windows PC

Put the enhanced CD in your computer CD drive and go to "My Computers." Double click on the CD icon where it says "TT Nonfiction" in order to play the audio stories. To view and print the pdf files, right click on the CD icon and select "Open." Then, all the pdf files will appear. Click to open a file and then print.

Download the CD into an Apple/Macintosh Computer

Put the enhanced CD into the VCD drive. Two pictures of the CD will appear on the desktop. (See figure 1.) Click on the CD labeled "Audio CD" and the storybook soundtracks will download to itunes. Use itunes to play each story from your Apple computer.

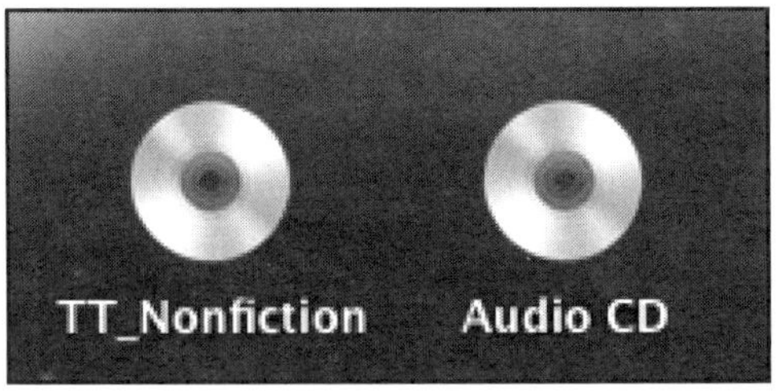

figure 1.

Click on the CD labled "TT_Nonfiction" and a folder will appear, labeled "Nonfiction PDFs Storybooks Activity Pages." (See figure 2.) Click on this folder and it will open to show you all the PDFs of the Storybooks and Activity Pages. (See figure 3.)

figure 2.

Click on the PDF of your choice and then print.

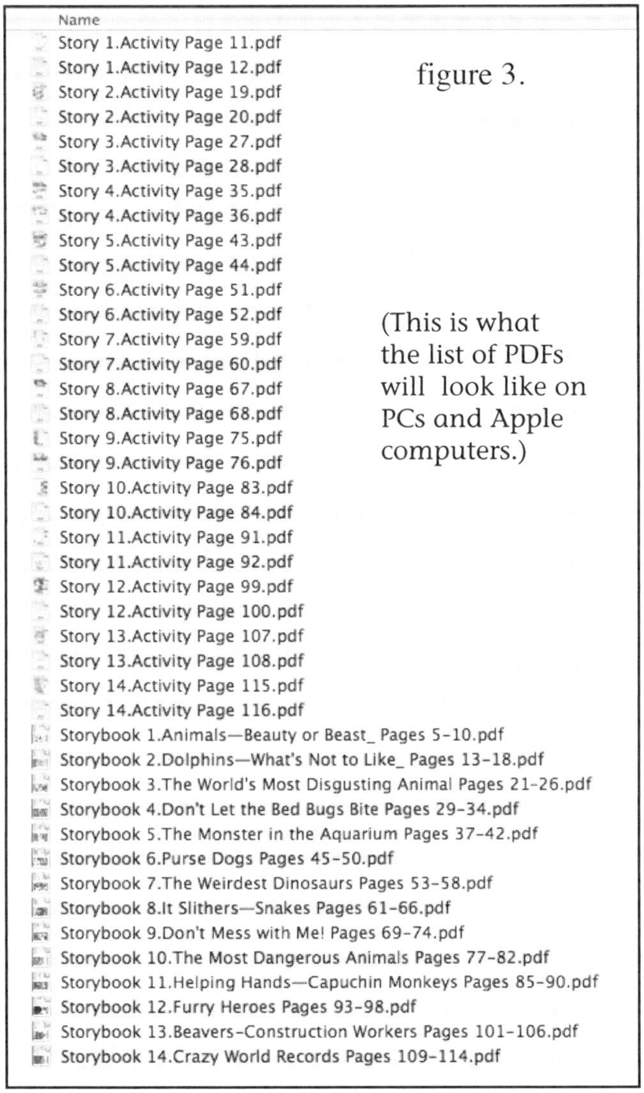

figure 3.

(This is what the list of PDFs will look like on PCs and Apple computers.)